OVERCOMING
ANXIETY

MO MYDLO

ANXIETY

SILOAM

Most Charisma House Book Group products are available at special quantity discounts for bulk purchase for sales promotions, premiums, fund-raising, and educational needs. For details, write Charisma House Book Group, 600 Rinehart Road, Lake Mary, Florida 32746, or telephone (407) 333-0600.

Overcoming Anxiety by Mo Mydlo
Published by Siloam
Charisma Media/Charisma House Book Group
600 Rinehart Road
Lake Mary, Florida 32746
www.charismahouse.com

Cover design by Justin Evans

Visit the author's website at unforsakenministries.com.

Library of Congress Cataloging-in-Publication Data:
Mydlo, Mo.
Overcoming anxiety / Mo Mydlo.
pages cm
Includes bibliographical references.
ISBN 978-1-62998-028-7 (trade paper) -- ISBN 978-1-62998-029-4 (e-book)
1. Anxiety--Religious aspects--Christianity. 2. Worry--Religious aspects--Christianity. 3. Trust in God--Christianity. I. Title.
BV4908.5.M93 2015
248.8'6--dc23
2015027623

While the author has made every effort to provide accurate Internet addresses at the time of publication, neither the publisher nor the author assumes any responsibility for errors or for changes that occur after publication.

15 16 17 18 19 — 98765432
Printed in the United States of America

I am blessed to dedicate this book to my husband, Tommy. Tommy's confidence in Christ, love of the Scriptures, and passionate desire to serve God has allowed me to be completely transparent with him for the past twenty-one years. This transparency has enabled God to heal me and put me in a place to help others. Tommy is a prince among men.

CONTENTS

ACKNOWLEDGMENTS

I WANT TO THANK my mom and dad for always encouraging my writing. Mom, your editing help is priceless, and Dad, your prayers for me while you're out on the tractor have never been ignored. You both have been the best parents anyone could ask for. Thank you for helping me to understand the unconditional love of God.

I want to thank my mother-in-law, Anne Marie, for being a shining example of a mother to me while my children were young and I was dealing with severe anxiety. Your love for me meant more than you will ever know.

To my precious children, Jacob, Travis, Sara, and Eli: If I never did another thing while on this earth than be your mommy, I will have been gloriously blessed. I completely adore you all. I pray daily for your future spouses and my future grandchildren, and for you to always pursue lives centered around Jesus Christ.

To my spiritual kids, Angel and Kurtis, I love you dearly. Every day since God has placed you in my and Tommy's lives, we have thanked Him for you.

To my sisters and brother: Thank you for always loving me—even when I was so self-righteous as a child that you nicknamed me "Mother Mo." We should have known back then I would be in ministry. Love you!

To the women at Unforsaken Women: Your dedication to me and to our precious once-a-month Thursday night women's event means more than I could say in words. Please know that when I wrote this book, I pictured many of your faces nodding and agreeing with me as I would type each word. Thank you for your love and support.

To the many pastors, Bible teachers, and authors from whom I have learned over the past sixteen years: Thank you. I owe much of my peace to your hard work and diligence in presenting the gospel to the nations.

INTRODUCTION

I AM ABOUT AN inch from being forty-two years old, and I can honestly say that the past forty-two years have taught me many lessons. But the best lessons I have learned have come in the past sixteen years spent devouring God's Word.

I have always been a worrier. Have you? Quite honestly I can't remember when I didn't struggle with anxiety. Did I know what it was? Not really. I remember my mom saying: "Maureen, stop worrying or you're going to give yourself an ulcer." Really all I think that did was make me worry about what an ulcer was. For my sweet mom who will read this, and mothers all over who will sometimes blame themselves for having a child with anxiety, may I please say to you: it's not your fault.

Sometimes anxiety cannot be pinpointed as to why we struggle with it, when we first noticed it, or if a traumatic event or series of events are what lead up to it. The truth is, sometimes two different children, raised in the same environment, under very similar circumstances will react differently to the same stimuli. That's at least what I have observed with my six siblings and myself. Pretty much half of us struggle with control issues and obsessiveness and anxiety, when the other half seems to allow life's struggles to roll off their backs pretty easily. Call it temperament, upbringing, or nature versus nurture, one half of the crew could be found quite often biting our fingernails, staring off during conversations, obviously dealing with other thoughts, with occasional bellyaches that led to frustration for my parents.

We moved a lot. I know some people would try to pin my anxiety on that. But, I remember worrying about things before we ever packed up the first moving van to start fresh in a new school or home. So that sort of negates that theory.

I vividly remember our first home. We had a sliding glass door off our family room. Because we lived on a hill, I could see all the way down the hill to the road that would lead to our house. It was starting to get dark, and I was worried about my dad. He was so special to me. As mom was cooking dinner, I kept asking her, "Where is Daddy?" "What if he is in an accident?" "What if he doesn't come home?" "Mommy, what if he is dead?"

My poor mother didn't know how to handle my anxiety. I was the first of her daughters to voice such continual concerns to her on a daily basis. My "what-ifs" must have been draining and concerning to her. After all, she had five children at the time to account for, much less answer all my dreadful questions. She did her best. But nothing seemed to ease my fear until I could visually see my father pull into the driveway with his truck. I would run out and greet him, throw my arms around him, and let it go. But the unhealthy closure I developed with situations such as this created more and more fears. My world was not peaceful until I felt some sort of control. This control was temporary and fleeting and somewhat contagious.

One fear grabbed the next fear, until I guess you could say I was chronically worried about everything.

I feared my parents getting a divorce, my parents dying, my parents starting to smoke (they weren't smokers, and my mother didn't even drink alcohol). I feared sickness, disease, and embarrassing situations such as head lice or vomiting in public. I feared letting my parents down in some way, not being perfect, not getting great grades or performing in a respectful manner. I feared everything that could possibly go wrong with our family. I loved my parents and my siblings so much that I think my immature, childlike thinking led me to believe that if I didn't worry about it, I didn't care enough.

Can you relate? I would venture to guess you can, otherwise you may not have bought a book about anxiety. I was a very worried child, and that child grew into a very worried teenager who developed defense mechanisms that could hide my fears in front of peers. I became obsessed with popularity and people pleasing. As long as I was popular and pleasing peers, my insecurity remained hidden. Only my closest family or friends knew I had mental issues that tormented me on a daily basis.

I praise God now that He gave me a very strong will. Many people would have given up and thrown in the towel if they had to live in my mind for any length of time. But God had me. He sustained me. He protected me from myself. He protected me from quitting, and I didn't even know Him yet. But He knew me.

By the time I was in high school my obsessive thinking and worry sort of morphed itself into a competitive spirit. I competed with everyone around me. I was jealous if anyone else got any attention. I harnessed my fears into competing for being president of every club I participated in. I had to be captain of every team I played on. I could not settle for second. I was president of my class for three years in high school. I organized every event our class participated in, and I somehow influenced enough people to vote for me for homecoming queen. As long as I was winning, my anxiety felt normal.

I was never truly secure enough in myself to go away to college. I lived at home and attended community college, but most of my friends left town and attended universities. They began experiencing the college life, and I became very depressed for the first time in a long time. The homecoming queen was used to having an entourage. All I had now were my studies and a lot of time to think. I had no one to compete with. I had no friends spending the night. I had no crowd around me to create the white noise I needed to drown the voices. Then guess who returned? My old enemy, anxiety.

I thank God now that I stayed home and attended community college, because it was there I found the love of my life, Tommy. That poor man had no idea what he was getting himself into. He saw a cute blonde with green eyes. Thank God he couldn't tell the future. I'm convinced that if he could he would have run immediately in the other direction. But God had us. He was writing our story.

Tommy and I were married very young. We had our first child, Jake, before we had been married for five months. Yes, you can do the math. We jumped right into each other's lives head on and never looked back. We did our best raising Jake. We were so young, it's like we grew up with him. Thank God he was an easy baby. But being a wife and mother opened up all new anxieties in my life. I had this little human to keep alive, and the minute-by-minute anxieties involved in that were dreadful to say the least. I was terrified of messing up. I loved Tommy and Jake so much. I was so afraid of letting them down.

I worked hard at becoming what I thought was the perfect mother. I was a helicopter mom. I hovered over him, wouldn't let people touch him unless they performed a medical scrub down before. I never left him. I obsessed over Jake so much that I began to ignore Tommy's needs. We rarely went on dates, and our sex life was few and far between. I was so tired from physically taking care of Jake all day and mentally trying to control anything that could ever harm him, I was purely exhausted every night. It was a miracle when we found out we were pregnant with our second child, Travis.

Travis and Jake became my life. I was a mom now, and I convinced myself that moms just worry. I actually fit in now. Moms were allowed to worry. I had a PhD in worry. I had done it my whole life, so now it was just focused on someone other than myself.

When my boys were three and one, I met a friend who introduced me to a MOPS (Mothers of Preschoolers) group. I attended and fell in love with MOPS. I met so many nice moms at this group, and my children developed some very sweet friends. We began to attend the church where the MOPS group was held. Tommy and I were raised in two different churches; Tommy was catholic, and I was protestant. We wanted our boys raised in church; after all, all of the books I was reading said it was good for the children. So we joined the church (for the kids). But God had other plans. Church was not for our children. Church was where we were going to meet Jesus.

A couple ladies from church invited me to my first Bible study. I declined several times, but then finally agreed to go. The funny thing is, I said yes because one of the ladies told me there was good coffee there. My friend, never question the power of a good cup of coffee.

These women taught me the Bible. They taught me about Jesus. One of them prayed the sinner's prayer with me, and I got saved. They taught me that anxiety and fear did not have to be my lot in life. These women at our Thursday afternoon Bible study helped God save my soul. I bought what they were selling and I have never looked back.

It wasn't until I had studied God's Word for a lengthy amount of time that I realized that anxiety, worry, and obsessive behaviors do not have to rule me. I can honestly tell you that I am free of Satan's strongholds that he once had on me. This freedom was made available to me only because I am a child of God. I think it's important that we remember that our stronghold of anxiety cannot always be pinpointed to a traumatic event or series of events. It doesn't always mean we have been abandoned, abused, neglected, or suffered some horrific event. I didn't have a perfect family or childhood, but it was a healthy and happy one. There is no perfect family, but there is a perfect God.

Sometimes our anxiety is simply a product of how God made us. Yes, we are fearfully and wonderfully made. The Word tells us this in Psalm 139:14. But I believe God created all of us with one tiny area in each of us that leaves us imperfect and draws us to a perfect God. He does this so that He will be glorified through our healing and our restoration. He does this because He loves us. He does this because He desires us to need Him.

In John 9:1–3 we read: "As Jesus passed by, He saw a man blind from birth. His disciples asked Him, 'Rabbi, who sinned, this man or his parents, that he was born blind?' Jesus answered, 'Neither this man nor his parents sinned. But it happened so that the works of God might be displayed in him'" (MEV).

We always desire an answer for why we struggle. We always want to make sense of God's story He is penning with our names written as the title. My friend, take heart if you cannot make sense of why you worry. God may be wanting to display His works in you. Praise God! May He have His way with us!

Whether you know why you have anxiety or not, make no mistake about it, God desires for you to pursue peace (1 Pet. 3:11). He desires for you to learn how to cast your cares on Him (Ps. 55:22). He desires for you to be still and know He is God (Ps. 46:10). He desires for you to allow your ashes to be made into something beautiful (Isa. 61:3). How do I know this? I have experienced it firsthand, and if that's not enough, God's Word says it is so.

The Lord is no respecter of persons, so I am 100 percent sure that the same freedom I have experienced is available to you. You will just need to work out your healing with a combination of prayer and studying God's Word. I have included in this book practical and spiritual tools and applications that you can use to overcome the stronghold of anxiety once and for all. Fighting to break down strongholds is a process—one that every believer in Jesus Christ has access to.

In each chapter of this book I will teach you a lesson. Please underline sentences, dog-ear pages, highlight ideas, and do whatever else you need to do to grasp the concepts included in each chapter. I would have no greater joy than to sign a copy of a book that looked like it made its way out of a battlefield. After all, this book is meant to help you fight the good fight of faith. I think the dirtier your Bible gets from use, the cleaner your heart will have become.

Read this book over and over if you need to. Sometimes the first time I read a book, I don't grasp all of the concepts God wants me to retain. It's only by flipping back to some of my highlighted areas a second time that I gain a better understanding of the concepts being taught. The same could be true for you.

At the end of each chapter you will have an opportunity to work through a homework section and to journal your feelings to the Lord. The journaling aspect of this process is crucial, as we must be transparent about our hurts and wrong thinking for God to truly heal us. We need to journal as if we don't want anyone to find it. God showed me one time, "You have to be real to get healed." If you have to journal your feelings to the Lord and then cross it all out in permanent marker, do so. Just get it out so you can break Satan's strength over you.

You will also be asked to meditate upon and memorize Scripture throughout this book, as you'll see that God's Word is the tool we need when fighting the ugly enemy of anxiety. You will become fluent in scriptures pertaining to the mind. Your new biblical knowledge will serve you well for the rest of your time here on earth.

I have included in each chapter reflections that were originally published on my blog *Unforsaken*, because that is one way I journal publicly. These reflections will help you see even more of my heart behind what I'm teaching. You see, I'm not perfect. But I serve a very perfect God whom I adore. I pray you will enjoy getting to know me better through these repurposed essays.

The most important thing that will happen to you through this book is that you will be invited to fall deeply in love with Jesus Christ. It is my heart's desire that He becomes your heart's desire. Proverbs 16:3 says, "Commit to the Lord whatever you do, and he will establish your plans." This is huge, my friend, and so important in your relationship with Jesus. Commit your every decision in life to Jesus. The word *commit* means "to put into charge, trust, entrust."[1] So this passage isn't saying, "Decide what you want, then wave your little God wand over it and you shall receive it." No, it is pretty much telling us, "Give God control of your everything, and watch your life change."

If only we could get that God's plans for us are exponentially better than anything we could ever plan for ourselves! He has our best interest in mind. He is our daddy. Jeremiah 29:11 says, "For I know the plans I have for you...plans to prosper you and not to harm you, plans to give you hope and a future." His plans are designed perfectly—and the truth is, anything that we could ever drum up for ourselves would only suffer in comparison.

We are God's handiwork. We are His clay, and He is the potter. We are the branches, and He is the vine. If it weren't for Him, we would wither up and die in our sins. He is the artist that paints every sunrise and sunset for our enjoyment. He is the giver of every good and perfect gift. He is the creator of our most-prized treasures, our spouses and our children. He is the provider of every piece of bread we put in our mouths. He is the healer of our bodies when we recover from a sickness. He is the author of every word written in the Bible, and the Bible is where we get our answers and the healing we desire. The Word is one of the main ways God communicates with us. We have to know it to know what He has to say.

Jesus takes full responsibility for our lives when we are devoted to Him. When we commit our lives to His perfect will and allow Him to govern them, we will truly succeed in this life as we prepare for our eternity with Him.

Dear friend, please hear my heart; I know anxiety is hard. Anxiety is excruciating sometimes. It can find you in the middle of a grocery store amongst a thousand people, in a crowded theatre, or alone in your living room. Anxiety does not discriminate. This ugly spirit can come on us when we least expect it. That is why I am going to teach you how to fight the good fight of faith. I am going to teach you how to live a life of trust. Some of us have never trusted another person in our lives, much less an invisible God, so this will not be easy. You will probably have good days and bad days until you can learn how to reach into your arsenal of knowledge and pull out the correct supernatural ammunition to fight this enemy effectively. Do not grow weary in this battle. You will be victorious. We are more than conquerors through Him who loved us (Rom. 8:37).

Our God is a God who heals! You will be better after you finish this book. That is my prayer for you.

Hide the Word in Your Heart

I once heard Beth Moore say, "I'm about three weeks from my next pit, should someone take away my Bible." When I heard her say that, I was moved to tears and wished I could have said to her, just like they would say on that old show *Name That Tune,* "I could name that tune in three notes," "Well, Beth, I am about three days from my next pit should someone take my Bible away."

I am desperate for the Word of God. I ache for it the minute I wake up. I yearn for it on days I have rushed into the day without ample time spent reading, meditating, and memorizing it.

I believe that God wants us desperate for Him. He didn't create us to be able to go it alone. He is that Daddy that desires that His kiddos stay right under His wing where He can watch us closely. And His Word is just like Him.

I want to ask you a question: What if the government stole our Bibles from us? Just all of a sudden, one day, just like in some other countries, the Bible became illegal. Have you hidden enough of the Word in your heart to fight off the enemy? Have you hidden enough of the Word in your heart to keep your mind set on things above? Have you hidden enough of the Word in your heart to keep your mind in perfect peace?

I've hidden a lot of it, but not enough. Not enough to withstand a day skipping time in my favorite chair with a cup of coffee, devouring the Word like food. Not enough to be able to say, "OK, I got this. I'm OK! I don't need to study." Oh, heck no! I am an ongoing, never-going-to-graduate-from-the-school-of-the-Word adult learner of the Good Book, and I always will be.

Yes, Beth Moore, I'm with you. Don't mess with my sword! I need it to fight.

Sorry, dear reader, if you were looking for a teacher who has it all together. Not this girl. But my Daddy does.

http://momydlo.wordpress.com/2014/01/24/hide-the-word-in-your-heart

Chapter 1

FIRST STEPS IN OVERCOMING

I AM SO HONORED that you decided to gear up for this study on overcoming anxiety biblically. I want to let you know that I could be considered somewhat of an expert on the study of anxiety. I have been memorizing and meditating on what God says about worry for sixteen years now. I have read countless books to feed my soul with truths to begin to recognize the lies that Satan and the world have fed me all of my life that has caused my anxiety. I have devoured sermons and teachings from countless psychologists, Bible teachers, and pastors. I pray you will understand that this is not a "get well quick" book. You have to do your homework. You have to pray and spend quality time with God. And most importantly and most agonizingly, you have to learn to wait on God.

First and foremost I think it would be good for me to say right off that I don't know why you have anxiety. Actually I don't know why I have anxiety either. I don't know why God chose for six kids to be born into the same household, be raised the same way, and be covered in love and support, yet for a couple of them never to struggle in their thinking while a few work through many mental strongholds.

Usually counselors want to hear about what has happened in your past that might have triggered the mental illness you are struggling with, but I am not going to go there with you. If you choose to go there with God, that is perfectly fine. I have walked it with Him in my own journey, and I keep coming to the same answer: *I don't know.*

You see, I was raised in a blessed family. We were loved, supported, encouraged, and cared for, yet I have always struggled with anxiety and obsessive behaviors. Call it an imbalance if you want. I believe it is what God uses to draw me close to Him.

Similarly I have observed my large family of nieces and nephews who have all been raised by two loving parents, encouraged in the Lord, and covered in God's grace—yet a few of them are little worriers while a few don't let anything bother them. I believe it is just a God thing that we may never understand this side of heaven. But I sure do love that I am able to minister to those sweet little worriers as I see them overthinking things as I had a tendency to do as a child. I am blessed to help them pursue the peace God designed them to live in, the peace that is captured only by covering yourself in the grace of God.

What I know is how to beat the anxiety with the tools God has shown me. Yes, if I hadn't struggled, I would have never reached for a life raft. But because I did, I can share it with you. I praise God for my struggles I once had because I am able to be used by Him now to love you deeply through the help you will find in this book.

It is important that you know everyone's deliverance in certain areas is dependent upon God's timing. I have witnessed God's healing and delivering power in people's lives that came both immediately as well as through a step-by-step process. God's healing can sometimes take place through the laying on of hands in prayer. Other times He speaks His healing plan to us through steps He asks us to take.

In her book *Finding Peace for Your Heart* Stormie Omartian writes, "If you sat in a dark closet all your life and suddenly hundreds of high wattage floodlights were turned on you, you would be blinded. It's the same way with deliverance. Too much light all at once would be difficult to manage. That's why deliverance must take place a layer at a time to match your growth in the Lord."[1] That's how it is for some of us—the freedom comes gradually, a layer at a time.

I know that's the case for me. God has been peeling away at my anxiety stronghold one layer at a time like an onion. If you had told me even a couple years ago that my days off from work would consist of complete quiet in the house, no plans on the horizon except a yearning for more and more of the Word of God, prayer, and time waiting to hear from Him, I would have thought you were crazy. Literally my goal now on my days off is to rest and spend quiet, uninterrupted time with God. But before I received my healing from God, I couldn't stand to be alone. I was so tormented by my flesh and by satanic attacks that I needed to be around people out of fear of myself. I was afraid to be alone. Now I ache for it. Praise God for deliverance!

Please know that my walk is ongoing and ever changing. God is not done with me, and I will not be completely healed until I am home with Him. We will always be working out our salvation with fear and trembling (Phil. 2:12).

So let's start here. Your first step to freedom from anxious thinking—and the most important step of all—is developing and growing your faith by spending needed time with God. Romans 10:17 says, "Faith comes by hearing, and hearing by the Word of God" (NKJV). Faith is a spiritual muscle that must be exercised, just as you work to develop muscles in your body. Without spending time working out, your body cannot develop muscles. Likewise, you cannot develop spiritual maturity and deliverance from your strongholds without spending time exercising your faith by studying the Word.

Have you been asking God for deliverance from worry? I know that I asked God so many times to just deliver me from worry and obsessive behaviors. I am quite sure that is why He shared 2 Corinthians 12:7–9 with me, which says, "To keep me from becoming conceited, I was given a thorn in my flesh, a messenger of Satan, to torment me. Three times I pleaded with the Lord to take it away from me. But he said to me, 'My grace is sufficient for you, for my power is made perfect in weakness.'" Believe me, friend, I asked God way more than three times to take my poor thinking patterns!

Again, sometimes God's deliverance doesn't come with a supernatural and miraculous healing, and that's most likely because He wants us to work out our healing and develop perseverance by exercising our faith. God's Word says in Hebrews 11:6, "Without faith it is impossible to please God, because anyone who comes to him must believe that he exists and that he rewards those who earnestly seek him." Are you diligently seeking Him? How much time are you spending with God?

It Takes Time

I remember when I first fell in love with my husband, Tommy. He made my heart skip a beat simply by calling me. He gave me goose bumps by the smell of his cologne and the sound of his car pulling in my driveway. I was enamored with him. Today after twenty-one years of marriage I can honestly say that yes, he still triggers my goose bumps sometimes, but that feeling suffers in comparison to that knowing I have in my heart that he is my partner for life. Those feelings are fun, but that knowing brings me joy. However, that knowing doesn't happen in the first few years of marriage. It grows from trust, and trust takes time.

In the same way developing our faith and trust in God takes time too, but it will give us that same kind of knowing:

That knowing
that we are loved.

That knowing
that we are protected.

That knowing
that we are delivered.

That knowing
that we are healed.

That knowing
that we are redeemed.

That knowing
that we are set free.

That knowing
that we are saved.

That knowing
that we are going to be OK.

That knowing
Requires faith

Faith is built on trust
And trust takes time to develop.

Let's get a little personal here. I'm going to ask you some questions. Can you tell me your name, address, phone number, and cell phone number? How many kids do you have? Are you married? What's your favorite color? What's your social security number, mother's maiden name, and the name of your elementary school?

All those questions start getting uncomfortable, right? We've been taught to protect ourselves in certain areas, and there are only a chosen few people you let into those precious places of knowledge. (My friend, don't give anyone those important numbers just because they ask you!)

My point is that we are guarded for certain reasons. My assistant, Jean, knows my house codes, the line items in my budget, and the safe word for picking up my son at school. She is in what you could call the circle of trust for the Mydlo family. But when I first met Jean, I would never have opened up to her with these innermost details that require a great amount of trust. It was only after spending a lot of time with her and getting to know her that I was able to trust her with all that I have.

Faith requires trust, and trust takes time. This means you need to spend time in God's Word in order to develop trust in Him. You will struggle to cast your cares on the Lord and let those cares go without developing trust in Him, and trust requires time—time in study, time meditating on the Word, time waiting on Him, and time rejoicing when He shows up.

I'm so grateful when God shows me how far I have come. My trust walk where anxiety is concerned is somewhat miraculous. It can only be explained by God's unrelenting love and grace in my life. I have teenage children now. With teenagers comes driving. My daughter, who sometimes in my mind seems as if I just dropped her off at kindergarten with braids in her hair, wearing her school uniform and her new squeaky sneakers, just drove my younger son to the store to run some errands. My life is in that car. My flesh and blood is in that car. How am I sitting here typing to you, fearless? I've learned to trust God with my most prized treasures: my children.

I've developed a trust walk that started with a crawl. After crawling, I took baby steps of trust, and now I am able to wholeheartedly go the distance with God. I've learned through time and perseverance to pray over my children and release them to God, trusting that He is their daddy and that He loves them even more than I could ever love them. I trust God simply because He has never let me down so far.

Does that mean all of my prayers have been answered with, "Sure, Mo, whatever you want"? No way! God has answered all of my prayers, but He hasn't always said yes. He has allowed me to experience hardships, persecution, pain, and offense, but He has been right there with me through it all. I trust a God who never leaves us to handle life alone. So yes, trusting God when you struggle with anxiety takes time, but it's worth it. I wouldn't trade a second of my journey for the peace I have now.

God wants us to confess to Him our deepest fears, anxieties, and thoughts we can share with no one else. He wants our time, our talents, our hearts, and our souls. He wants our desires, our dreams, our joys, and our sorrows. He wants us to go to Him with everything. And because He knows we most likely won't do that on our own, sometimes He allows us to deal with things such as anxiety, depression, or obsessive behaviors to draw us closer to Him out of our desperation.

Your God-Shaped Hole

Everyone born on this earth has a thorn in their flesh like the Apostle Paul talked about. Everyone has what I like to refer to as their "God-shaped hole." We are made in God's image, but He leaves one small hole inside us that only He can fill. For some people, that thorn is a habit or addiction. For some people, it is procrastination or timidity. For others, it may be their mouths. I may never get to meet you this side of eternity to ask, but can I wager to bet that your God-shaped hole is anxiety? Mine is. It always has been. The more I think about it; I am convinced that I was born this way, imperfect and flawed, magnetically attracted to a perfect Healer, Redeemer, Restorer, Savior, and Love, Jesus Christ.

It took me twenty-two years without a relationship with Christ, coping with my anxiety and developing defense mechanisms to simply fit in when I felt like such an outcast deep down, to realize God wants to be the only one I turn to with my anxiety so that He can fill me. He allows us to have those struggles so He can be glorified in us when we become well. He's it! He's the only sure fit for our holes.

I want to tell you this right now so you will know you aren't alone: everyone has a God-shaped hole. *Everyone!* We just try to fill it with different things. Some try to fill it with shopping or busyness. Some try to fill it with their jobs or maybe even church work. We may try to fill that hole with friendships and pleasures, habits or hang-ups. For those of us with anxiety, we may try to fill that hole up by numbing it with drugs. You may even be taking some drugs for anxiety right now, but you are still feeling empty. I can almost promise you this, that hole will never feel totally full until we allow the God of the universe to fill that void. Please note, I am not advocating you stop taking your medication that has been prescribed for you. You should always seek the help of a medical professional should you decide you are ever ready to wean yourself off any medication.

Now let's look at God's solution. In John 4 we meet the woman at the well. Jesus encounters this Samaritan woman, approaches her, and asks her for a drink. It is a gross understatement to say that His reaching out to her caught her off guard. She was not expecting to speak with anyone that day, much less a Jewish man. Because of the intense prejudice and the class systems of the day, Jews did not associate with Samaritans, and Jewish men did not speak to women when their husbands were not present. So Jesus's reaching out to this woman caught her out of her expected element.

And Jesus says to her, "Will you give me a drink?" When Jesus asks this woman for a drink of water, we have to remember one thing: Jesus is God. He was there with God the Father at the creation of the earth. He is all-powerful, omnipotent, omnipresent, and able to do whatever He wants when He wants. Do you really think He needed a drink? I feel like when Jesus asked that question, He was really saying, "Can we talk?"

So Jesus speaks with the woman about her past husbands and how the man she is with now isn't even her husband. She is obviously amazed that He knows her life's innermost details.

Then Jesus decides to talk to her about living water and says that if she drinks from this living water, she will never grow thirsty again. He starts explaining that we don't worship at a place; rather, we live a life of worship. He says God is a Spirit being, and we must worship Him in Spirit and in truth. We have to worship Him with our days, our nights, our hearts, our minds, our everything.

He's trying to get her to see He is it! He is the living water that will never go dry, the love relationship that will never leave you aching for more, the friend that sticks closer than a brother, the only lover who will never let you down, the only way to heaven, the cure for your heartache, the peace for any situation, the healer of your broken heart, the perfect love you are searching for and never finding. He is it! It's Him!

You see, Jesus exposed this woman's God-shaped hole. And we are all built with that same small hole on the inside that only God can fill. He built us to need Him. He built us to be desperate for Him. And until we fill that hole with Him, something deep on the inside of us always knows we are incomplete. On our best days here on earth—the sun shining, the bank account full, the family well, the moon and stars aligning perfectly—we realize that without Jesus, something is still missing. And if we don't recognize that He's the only thing designed to fill that hole, we try to fill it with other things. We may try:

- Accumulating wealth
- Shopping for more stuff
- Storing up treasures around us
- Searching for love in all the wrong places
- Taking something to numb the ache
- Working ourselves to exhaustion to quiet the voices
- Pursuing goals and dreams that still leave us feeling empty

Until we realize that our God-shaped hole can only be filled with a love relationship with Jesus, we create little gods to worship and bow down to. God built us to worship, we become involved in idolatry, and we usually don't even know we are doing it! Idolatry is defined as extreme admiration, love, or reverence for something or someone. A lot of the time when our flesh feels good in some way, our deceitful hearts are drawn toward that feeling over and over, whether it is good for us or not.

In the case of anxiety we are often so tired of not feeling quite right in our thinking that when something provides an immediate, though not lasting, result, we sometimes exalt these things. We promote these things. We endorse these things. We idolize these things. Our hearts are like little idol manufacturers. The truth is, these idols may provide temporary help but they ultimately prevent our long-term healing from happening, because we have taken our eyes off our true God, Jesus Christ.

Personally I remember when my two boys were very young. I hadn't yet accepted Christ, and I was intensely struggling with anxiety. Shopping at the mall would make me feel pretty good for a little while. I reasoned I was taking the boys on an outing, I was exercising walking around the mall, and I was being a good mother purchasing every toy my boys could ever desire and more overalls than any two toddlers could ever wear.

If we didn't have the money, I would put it on the credit card. Then when that credit card was full, I would apply for a new one or extend my credit. It didn't take long to realize that I was in a very dangerous situation financially. My husband and I had accumulated a massive amount of credit card debt, and I had nothing to show for it but stuff I didn't need, guilt I couldn't shake, and my anxiety that of course still loomed in the background as always.

The time that I should have been spending immersed in God's Word, praying to Him for comfort, confessing truths out loud to myself, loving God and loving my kids, was replaced with the idol of shopping and debt spending. It was a very costly idol that was dedicated to my family's financial destruction. My temporary high demanded a high cost.

When Jesus says, "Everyone who drinks this water will be thirsty again" (John 4:13), He is so right. Everyone who drinks of the well of idolatry—which pretty much means putting anything ahead of your relationship with

Christ—will keep needing more, because that thing you idolize lacks Jesus. Jesus is perfectly designed to fit into all of our God-shaped holes. We need to trust Jesus and stop panning for gold in the empty wells of life, as they will only leave us wanting for more.

Are You Willing to Work?

If you are reading this book, then anxiety, obsessive thinking, and worry are most likely a few of the God-shaped holes in your heart. You are probably sick and tired of your own stinkin' thinkin' or you wouldn't have kept reading past the dedication page. You must be completely fed up with days of Satan stealing your peace and joy, or you would have bought a different type of book.

I am going to tell you something. You can beat this—but it's going to take a lot of work. The God I love and have become close friends with has allowed me to witness Him performing many miracles. However, when it comes to the renewing of our minds, He usually wants us to do a little homework. There are drugs you can take to numb yourself, and I am sure some of you have taken them or are taking them still. But if those drugs were working, you wouldn't still be seeking something else, would you? Please don't think I'm advocating going off medication if your doctor has prescribed it. I am simply telling you to give the Great Physician some room to work in your life. As Charles F. Stanley says in *Confronting Casual Christianity*, "Relinquish all claims to your life. Lay aside the easy road, the pathway of convenience...away with a bogus brand of Christianity that does not issue a clarion call for commitment."[2]

There are countless scriptures in God's Word that help to combat worry. You have to become very acquainted with these scriptures to fight the good fight of faith. If you do your work, then your Bible should start opening of its own accord to all of the dog-eared, underlined pages in it. What I mean is, your Bible needs to get a little dirty. I don't mean dusty. I mean there need to be some tear stains in it from you crying out to God on those pages. There need to be some coffee stains on those necessary scriptures because the second you stumbled your way to the coffee pot in the morning, you knew you'd better grab that Bible and get in your favorite chair to study the Word. Your Bible better start swelling up and expanding like mine has. I don't know how it happened. I just go with it! I'm pretty sure I dropped it in the pool or the tub too many times.

If you can't tell already, I am going to challenge you to step it up. You may already have your daily devotion time each day, and you are still not feeling free. Maybe you spend each morning praying for the people on the prayer chain but you haven't felt any of those prayers coming through for you. Maybe you turn on Christian music in your home but you just can't seem to feel worshipful. Maybe you have heard countless pastors say from the pulpit how anxiety is not appropriate for God's people, and we are called to have faith instead of fear, and you are wondering why you still feel chained up in your thinking.

There is a next step always. We have to learn that our walk is just that, a walk. We put one foot in front of the other, and we have to keep moving. If you are reading from a devotional, I want to encourage you to memorize the scriptures it covers. If you are praying for those people on the prayer chain, try getting out of your comfy chair and onto your knees. Even better, if your health will allow it, get on your face. If you don't feel like you are worshipping when you are hearing those worship songs that come across the radio, try dancing to them. How about every time you are tempted to feel condemned when the pastor preaches faith not fear, you bow your head, repent, and say, "Show me how, Lord"?

God is not trying to catch you looking dumb. He wants to catch you looking desperate. He wants you desperate enough for peace that you will make Him number one. He wants you desperate enough to wake up before the rest of your family, when it's still dark, and sit with Him outside and watch the sunrise He created. He wants you desperate enough that you will put that annoying cell phone on silent and talk to the only One who has any real advice for you that will last. He wants you desperate enough that instead of calling your husband or girlfriend all day long to tell them your troubles, you will tell Him.

Psalm 55:22 says, "Cast your cares on the LORD and he will sustain you; he will never let the righteous be shaken." That is a pretty serious promise. If we truly believe that God's Word is 100 percent truth, then we need to believe His promises—that if you cast your cares on Him, He will sustain you and won't let you fall. God doesn't break His promises. He can't lie. Numbers 23:19 says, "God is not human, that he should lie, not a human being, that he should change his mind." We need to grasp how serious God is about asking us not to carry our own burdens. He wants to take them from us. We have to hand them over.

Think about it this way. Do you have small children who go to school? Do you remember that first day of school for them when you had to bring in that enormous amount of school supplies for the entire year? Why is it that we don't put those precious little ones on the bus their first day? We fill up that car rider line so full that school starts a half-hour late because of all the drop-offs. We do it because we are the moms and dads. We don't want our little ones trying to carry that immense load into school themselves. We carry it for them.

In the same way God is our Father, and He doesn't want us carrying all our burdens on our own, either. Just as it would break our hearts as parents to open the front door of the house and nudge our kids down the road to school with too much for their little arms to carry, it breaks God's heart when we try to go it alone. We disappoint the Holy Spirit when we think we're supposed to be superheroes of our own lives.

I'm sure you're familiar with the verse 1 Peter 5:7, "Cast all your anxiety on him because he cares for you." This verse reminds me of how my husband gets so upset with me when I don't ask him for help with things such as the lawn or the pool. I love working around the house, so it really doesn't bother me to tackle those kinds of things. But even though I know Tommy is so much better at caring for those things than I am, I still decide to handle it myself. Sometimes things actually end up broken because I try to carry what I really don't have the strength to carry. Sometimes a job needs to be redone because my way of doing it really wasn't the most efficient way. I need to let go of my pride and ask for help with the house, just as we need to give God the burdens of our lives that He wants to carry for us. He is much better at it than we are.

God cares for us as His children. He is not interested in our trying to be independent of Him. He is interested in us sharing everything we are with Him. He says to cast all our anxiety on Him, and *all* means *all.*

Through the reading of this book, I pray you will develop new habits of casting your cares on the Lord, of giving God your burdens, and of throwing off the sin that so easily entangles you in the lies that Satan wants you to keep believing—lies that may sound something like, "You'll never get better," "No one thinks like you," and "You can never tell anyone you think like this." Or maybe deceptions such as, "You are a terrible mom, wife, or woman," "You're never going to heaven," or "I bet you're not even saved."

Please understand this: *Satan is the father of lies.* It says in John 10:10, "The thief comes only to steal and kill and destroy," but the next line is a promise from God: "I have come that they may have life, and have it to the full." Jesus came to give you life in abundance.

It Comes Down to Love

I want to give you a tiny crash course in the love of God. Bear with me here, because in order to place your full trust in Him, you need to be educated in how much He loves you. This may sound very kindergarten, Sunday school, or elementary school level to you, but dear friend, God is love. Say it to yourself: *God is love.* Now I didn't say God is loving, though of course He is. I said God is love. He is the very essence of love. If you want to know what love is, study God. If you want to get to know God, study the word *love*. You can test it both ways. Literally anywhere you see the word *God* in the Bible, you can replace His name word with the word *love*, and it will work the same.

For example, in thinking about John 3:16, we could say, "Love so loved the world that love gave His one and only love, so that whoever believeth in love shall not perish but have eternal life." That's true love right there. Now let's do the opposite with a different scripture. In 1 Corinthians 13:4–8 let's put God's name everywhere we see the word *love*. It would look like this:

> God is patient, God is kind. God does not envy, God does not boast, God is not proud. God does not dishonor others, God is not self-seeking, God is not easily angered, God keeps no record of wrongs. God does not delight in evil but rejoices with the truth. God always protects, always trusts, always hopes, always perseveres. God never fails.

Yes, it truly works.

In the Bible the disciple John has so much confidence in how much Jesus loved him, he called himself "the disciple whom Jesus loved" (John 13:23). I want to have that sort of confidence in God's love for me. Don't you too? The truth is, though, that the devil has lied to me so many times throughout my life, telling me how messed up I am and that Jesus can't truly love me like I need Him to. I have had to take some lessons from St. John to build my confidence. John had no problem recognizing Jesus's love toward him because he had Jesus proving it over and over right in front of his very eyes. Once we begin to trust Jesus with our entire lives, we will also recognize ourselves as the "disciples whom Jesus loves." I want this for you!

We need to recognize the love God has for us because it is that love that grows our trust, and once we can trust God completely, fear gets eradicated. We need to memorize and renew our minds to the truth in 1 John 4:18: "There is no fear in love. But perfect love drives out fear." Since God is love, we can simply see that "perfect God casts out fear"! Please realize how much you are loved. Then trust in that love to take away your fear.

Start Here

I'll be up front with you and say that the very first step in your healing from anxiety is to pursue a relationship with Christ. If you have not yet made a decision to follow Jesus, you must do so in order to inherit eternal life and receive the blessings that come from that relationship with Him. The Word says, "Everyone who calls on the name of the Lord will be saved" (Rom. 10:13). You need to accept Jesus and make Him Lord of your life first. It's the initial step toward the healing you ultimately seek.

The decision to make Jesus Lord of your life is literally the most important decision you will ever make. Once you make this decision, the Bible says that there is a party going on in heaven. Luke 15:10 says, "Likewise, I tell you, there will be more joy in heaven over one sinner who repents than over ninety-nine righteous men who need no repentance" (MEV). The angels are leading the celebration. You become sealed for redemption in that moment, so when you take your last breath, your eternal residence in heaven is secured.

After that, if you have not confessed your sins to God, you need to get very real with Him. Tell Him everything. He knows it already. He's just waiting for you to lay it down.

Thankfully because of the precious blood shed by Jesus on the cross, we no longer are responsible for our inability to be forgiven completely of our sins. God's work of salvation and the complete atonement once and for all for our sins was finished at that moment, and Jesus's blood is what finished it. He was the final and ultimate sacrifice for all of our sins of the past, our sins today, and our sins of the future. When Jesus said, "It is finished," He meant business. He wanted us to know the perfect atonement has been made, the work has been done, the trial is over. We are guilt free, our debt of sin is paid, and we are more than conquerors in Him.

I am going to tell you right now that healing is one of the finished works of Jesus Christ at the cross. Healing is available to us today because of what Jesus did two thousand years ago. I didn't make it up. It's in the Word. That healing includes mental healing as well. Isaiah 53:5 says, "But he was pierced for our transgressions, he was crushed for our iniquities; the punishment that brought us peace was on him, and by his wounds we are healed."

The next step may be the hardest: repentance. Repentance means deciding to turn from your sins, leave them behind, and start your new life with Jesus at the lead. To elaborate, I'm going to go out on a limb here and ask you a question. Do you think it makes God excited to see us struggling in strongholds, habits, hurts, and physical, mental, and emotional pain when He had to witness His Son's death in order for us to be free of those things? I'm going to answer my own question with a resounding no! I'm sure it grieves Him greatly. If we want physical healing or healing of strongholds of the mind or healing from addictions or habits or generational curses, we have to draw a blood line in the sand and say to the devil, "No more, devil! I'm not living like this anymore, and I am not passing this fear on to my children."

Then, finally, comes baptism. Baptism represents the death, burial, and resurrection of our Lord, Jesus Christ. Baptism can be one of those doctrinal issues that divides the church. The simple truth is that Jesus was baptized, and if we are His disciples, we do what He did, so we are baptized too.

These are, of course, the first steps to freedom in Christ.

After you make the decision to make Jesus Lord of your life and follow it up with confession, repentance, and baptism, it is up to you to do your homework, study the Word, memorize the Word, and fall in love with the Word. That's where this book takes you next. And let me tell you, in the homework and journaling time you spend while working through this book, I would encourage you to be very transparent. Wounds from past and present hurts do not heal by shoving them down deep and burying them alive. We must allow air to get to them so that God can heal them completely.

So let's dive in.

Some Trust in Chariots

This morning, I was outside on my deck with my coffee, praying, and as I closed my eyes and listened to the birds singing and the bugs buzzing, I kept hearing a faint beeping in between the sounds of nature. It was a nagging, consistent beep that was stealing my attention. It didn't take long for me to realize that it was my neighbor's security system.

I was immediately in prayer for them. I walk by their house, and I hear that beep, and I see the outdoor cameras and the signs that say that this house is under video surveillance, and it makes me sad for them. I know they must struggle with fear. The house is always so tightly shut up—no open blinds, no screened door open to let in the light, no sounds of nature echoing into their house.

It reminds me of a time in my life when I tried to control every situation around me to protect myself and my loved ones so much that I blocked out the beauty that now radiates through our home. It reminds me of a time that I was afraid to take walks alone or be home alone at night. It reminds me of a time I was gripped with fear because I was absent of the Holy Spirit.

Do we lock our doors at night? Of course! Christians must use wisdom as well as live a life of faith. But do I believe those locks are what protect me? Heck no! I know that Jesus Christ is the protector of our home. I believe that when evil even thinks of stepping on our lawn, legions of angels gear up, ready to fight for us. I believe that God didn't give us the sounds of nature and the beauty of the outdoors for us to watch through tiny peepholes. I believe that God fights for those who trust in Him.

The Word says in Psalm 20:7, "Some trust in chariots and some in horses, but we trust in the name of the LORD our God." I use wisdom in protecting my family and home, but I don't put my trust in those things. I put my trust in God. You see, until I learned to do that, none of the cheap substitutes I used to trust in would bring me peace. Only trusting in God's protection gives me the peace that the Bible describes as passing all understanding (Phil. 4:7). Can I explain why I have that peace now? Nope. It's supernatural because it is from Him.

When I see those stickers that say, "This home is protected by..." I always want to put a sticker on my windows that says, "This home is protected by God." I wouldn't want to mess with that security system! Some trust in chariots and horses, but I trust in the name of Jesus Christ.

http://momydlo.wordpress.com
/2014/06/29/some-trust-in-chariots

Homework

Spend some time in prayer as you answer the following questions.

1. *Why must we spend quality time with God?*

2. *How can we truly begin to trust God?*

3. Where are you not fully trusting God?

4. What steps can you take to develop more intimate time with Him?

5. In what ways do you know you are loved by God? When do you feel loved by Him?

Read the following scriptures and write them out in your own words:

- Proverbs 3:5–6

- Proverbs 3:21–26

- Proverbs 20:7

- Proverbs 29:25

- Romans 10:17

- 1 Peter 5:7

- Psalm 55:22

Memorize

Trust in the Lord with all your heart
  and lean not on your own understanding;
in all your ways submit to Him,
  and He will make your paths straight.
—Proverbs 3:5–6

Confession

Practice saying out loud over and over this week: "I am loved by God. He is my friend who sticks closer than a brother."

Application

Make a date with God each day and keep it! Make a commitment to spend each day this week with the lover of your soul, Jesus. Put it on the calendar if need be. Pursue Him. He is pursuing you.

Journal Time

Focus on talking to God like your best friend as you journal. Tell Him about whatever is weighing on your mind. I promise He is just waiting to take it from you.

Chapter 2

CASTING DOWN IDOLS

I LOVE MY HOUSE. We have lived in this four-bedroom ranch house on a cul-de-sac for over fourteen years now. I say joyfully, "God willing, my grandbabies will eat family dinners here at this home." This home has seen some family get-togethers. We love having family and friends here to share in the blessing that God has given us of a safe, welcoming home. This home has hosted Sunday dinners, holiday parties, trick-or-treating hayrides, two of my four children's graduation parties, as well as several Fourth of July picnics with cars parked up and down the street. Tommy and I celebrated our twentieth anniversary party here, and countless birthday candles have been extinguished in our kitchen.

I have designed each room in this home, and I've painted the interior and exterior countless times shoulder to shoulder with my hubby as he graciously understood when I was just "ready to paint again." My kitchen alone has been four different colors in fourteen years, which averages a new makeover every three and a half years. I get away with it only because I am such a thrifty shopper, and I love taking pieces that people are ready to discard and repurposing them to make something new. I love mowing the lawn, trimming the hedges, cleaning the garage, napping in my porch swing, and writing messages and books from the side of my aboveground pool. I am a homebody.

But about two months ago God started chipping away at something in me related to this house. It's like that between us. Just when I am spiritually naked and exposed enough, God removes another one of my old fleshy layers, like that onion I mentioned in the last chapter.

Here's how it happened.

I kept thinking about my house during my prayer time and wondering, "What could we sell this house for?" I immediately was almost rebuking myself every time I would think about it. I would say to myself, "I don't want to move. Why am I even thinking about this?" Then the next time I would pray, I would think, "Well, perhaps we have enough equity in our house to pay off all our debt and build a smaller house on more land and have no mortgage." Then I would shake my head again, not even wanting to go down that road.

This struggle went on for about a week, until I realized God was testing my heart. Once I realized it was a test, I went straight to my knees and confessed to God that whatever He would ask me to do I would do it, no questions asked, no matter how hard the change would be for me.

Tommy and I prayed it over, and we decided to contact a Realtor friend of ours and see if this was God's plan for us. We reasoned that if the market was at the point that we could financially sell our house and become debt free, including a new home that we would live in, then this may be God trying to bless us, and we didn't want to miss that.

Our friend offered to help us by doing a market analysis, seeing where our house compared to other homes and if it would be a smart time for us to make a change. While she worked, I prayed. I prayed, and I looked at other places we could live in that are in my children's school district. I prayed about building a home or buying an existing home, or perhaps a condo. Tommy and I prayed separately and together about this decision while we waited for our friend's advice.

While we talked in bed one night, I turned to him and said with a lump in my throat, "Honey, I don't want to move."

He said, "We don't have to move, Mo."

I said to him, "Yes, babe, if God calls us to move, we have to move. I will not allow this home to be an idol to me."

He hugged me, and we went to sleep.

The next morning, I received a call from our Realtor friend. She seemed almost nervous to tell me the news she had for me. She said, "Mo, we could sell your house and get this amount, and you could definitely be in a good place, but I would suggest you wait a couple of years to sell for the market to improve some more, and you would be in a great place."

I thanked her and said, "I have to be honest with you. I am happy. I didn't want to move, but if God was moving us, I wanted to be obedient."

You see, I really didn't think God wanted us to give up our home. I think He was just testing my heart to see if I would. And that, my friend, gets us talking about the issue of idolatry.

What Do You Worship?

God specifically talks about his hatred for idolatry in the Book of Exodus, saying:

> You shall not make for yourself an image in the form of anything in heaven above or on the earth beneath or in the waters below. You shall not bow down to them or worship them; for I, the LORD your God, am a jealous God, punishing the children for the sin of the parents to the third and fourth generation of those who hate me, but showing love to a thousand generations of those who love me and keep my commandments.
>
> —EXODUS 20:4–6

Let's connect the dots between idolatry and the anxiety struggle. First, in chapter 1 we talked about the seriousness of spending quality time with the Lord. Prayerlessness is a surefire way to keep yourself in bondage to fear. Until you realize that prayer is your lifeline in times of trouble, you will keep searching in other areas to fill that void. And you will continue to be disappointed. The Bible calls those other areas that you turn to idols. You need to cast down those idols when you recognize them, and if you cannot recognize them, you need to ask God to reveal the areas in your life where you substitute other things for Him.

Prayer opens up a relationship between you and the living God. Prayer is how we voice our struggles to God so that He can take them and release us from them. So often we will pick up the phone to call a friend when we are worried, we scroll through a newsfeed when we need to get our minds off our problems or we post a thought to an unidentifiable group of "friends" on social media when God is right there ready to help. God needs to be our first call. We call on Him through prayer. When we call on anything else before Him, we flirt with idolatry. Teach yourself this rhyme to avoid jumping to another defense mechanism before you consult with Christ: "When I fear, I need God here. Who needs to hear it? Holy Spirit." Then drop to your knees, bow your head, or simply whisper "Help me, Jesus." You will be amazed how fast He runs to you. You can feel good at that point because you involved God first and avoided idolatry.

Now, just like the example I shared with you about my house, idols are not necessarily graven images that people have created out of wood or cement. They can be possessions, and they can be addictions and habits such as smoking, drinking, shopping, or food. They can even be our children or our husbands. They can be television or the Internet. Whatever you are turning to to calm your nerves or lighten your load, if it is not Jesus, it could become an idol.

As someone with a history of anxiety, I am constantly protecting my heart from idolatry. Routines and consistency, as well as predictable situations, are positive things, but they can be potential idols for me since I am naturally obsessive. Maybe you can relate. But you know what I've learned? God loves me too much to allow me to bow down to these idols. I have to be willing to cast down any earthly thing that binds me from fulfilling God's perfect purposes in my life, and I have to be willing to loose the peace that comes from trusting only Him as the one true God in my life. God wants this for you too.

When it comes to our response, I think it is easy to spot idols, a little harder to cast them down, then harder still figuring out how to get some peace, even if it is temporary, after you have been obedient. We need replacement therapy. We have to replace our fears, anxieties, defense mechanisms, and controlling behaviors with prayer,

Scripture, meditation, and thanksgiving. This is because our brains will not stop thinking about something just because we told it to. We must replace our negative thinking and behaviors with something else.

Let me demonstrate this. Close your eyes. Think about the letter x. OK, now write the letter x with your finger in the air. Make an x in your mind, then say the letter x. Say it again. Picture that x in your mind again. OK, stop. Don't think about x. No more thinking about x. Can you just stop? No, of course not. But what do you do with x now? It doesn't just go away or fall out of the alphabet because you want it to. How do you deal with x? You must replace x with y.

In the same way something has to replace your anxious thought or it will continue to play in your mind. Our minds are like computers, and they process what is downloaded into them.

So what is your y supposed to be? Let me tell you. If we make y anything except the Word of God, prayer, praise, or thankfulness, it can become an idol in our lives—and that is a dangerous place to be.

Many people have made their cell phones their y. They don't know how to get into a quiet car without dialing someone to converse with on the way. Maybe you feel you have to stay plugged into things such as social media because reading about other people's lives and misadventures gets your mind off your own. I know most of us love social media. Kept at a healthy level, it can be a very useful and fun thing. But make sure you are not making it your idol. If you get on the computer during the day because you feel lonely and need to feel connected to someone, try praying and spending time in God's Word first. Avoid falling into a trap of idolatry.

There are so many things we try to make our y because we have to get our minds off x. X is killing our moods, robbing our peace, and putting an ulcer in our stomachs, so we pick a quick y to replace it. J. Keith Miller states in *Hope in the Fast Lane: A New Look at Faith in a Compulsive World*, "So by engaging in certain compulsive behaviors (working compulsively, eating too much, drinking too much, taking tranquilizers, engaging in compulsive sexual thoughts and behaviors, being addicted to people-pleasing or even church work), we can 'fill our lives' and avoid facing our feelings, our sins, and our deepest reality—that God could use in our lives to help us see ourselves and grow spiritually."[1]

What is your y? Is it debt-spending, talking to friends, gossip, drugs, or food? We all try other y's to replace our x's, but the truth is, they all leave us empty and desiring something more. Philippians 3:7–8 says, "But whatever were gains to me I now consider loss for the sake of Christ. What is more, I consider everything a loss because of the surpassing worth of knowing Christ Jesus my Lord, for whose sake I have lost all things. I consider them garbage, that I may gain Christ." Whatever you cast down for Christ, no matter what it means to you, could never compare to the peace that passes all understanding, which is exactly what God's Word will give you if you learn to apply it to your life.

When the Word of God is used to conquer worry, you will recognize the amazing and powerful obsession that you will gain for more and more of the Word in your life. Just as an addict craves more and more of a drug to get a

e you recognize the power of the Word of
your life, the more you will want to apply
your life, and you will begin to live in that
with God.

Begin With the Word

So how do you start? The first thing you need to do is find scriptures in the Bible that pertain to casting your cares on Christ, overcoming fear, renewing your mind, and anxiety. Write them all in your journal. Many Bibles, especially teaching or student Bibles, have a concordance. The concordance lists specific words found throughout the Scriptures. It is located between the Book of Revelation and the back cover of your Bible. Look up words such as *fear*, *worry*, *mind*, and *think*, and write them out.

If your Bible doesn't have a concordance, search online for scriptures like this. Many Bible sites are available to search by verse, topic, or keywords in whatever version of the Bible or language you prefer. Or better yet, ask a sister in Christ to give you a few scriptures to start with. As you dig deeper into God's Word, you will find these treasures for yourself, hidden in God's glorious gift to us of His Word.

Now you will need to memorize these scriptures. Yes, I know, we don't love memorizing, but there is no way around it. In order to call on the Word, you need to know it. Most likely there will be very few occasions that allow you the time or place to say, "Oh, wait! Let me go get my Bible and look up something to combat that thought!" We need to be prepared. Psalm 119:11 says, "I have hidden your word in my heart that I might not sin against you." We need to hide God's Word in our hearts through memorization. We all do what is important to us. Believe me when I say memorizing Scripture is important.

Put Scripture to memory in whatever way works for you. One way that works for me is to write out index cards and carry them with me or post them in places where I spend a lot of time. You can put them on the bathroom mirror, the car dash, or on your desk by the phone. You can prop them up at the sink as you do the dishes, stick them to the wall as you clean the kids' rooms, or bring them to the table as you eat your lunch. If you are an auditory learner, record scriptures as a note to yourself in your phone and make a goal of playing it ten times during the day.

Here's what you do next. The minute you feel an anxious thought come to mind, cast down that thought immediately by saying, "I leave that thought at the cross." Actually visualize yourself placing that thought on the ground at Jesus's feet. Remember, God calls us to cast our cares on Him, for He cares for us (1 Pet. 5:7). When we cast our cares on Jesus, our thinking doesn't get carried away or out of control. Second Corinthians 10:5 says, "We demolish arguments and every pretension that sets itself up against the knowledge of God, and we take captive every thought to make it obedient to Christ." After you leave that thought at the cross, you must not pick it back up. Casting it down is x. The y is up to us in knowing the truths in God's Word.

Often I will cast a thought at the foot of Jesus and say out loud to myself, "I leave it at the cross," while actually drawing a cross in the air to remind myself that I am not to pick it back up. Depending on what the thought is, I confess the Word of God to myself, calling on any scriptures that I can think of at the time.

For example, when I find myself fearful, I might say:

- "God has not given me a spirit of fear, but of power, might, and a sound mind" (2 Tim. 1:7).
- "There is no fear in love; perfect love casts out fear" (1 John 4:18).
- "God's Word is a lamp to my feet and a light to my path" (Ps. 119:105).
- "For I know the plans I have for you, says the Lord. Plans to prosper you and not harm you; plans to give you hope and a future" (Jer. 29:11).
- "The Lord is my rock and my redeemer" (Ps. 19:14).
- "Do not fear, for I am with you!" (Isa. 41:10).
- "Even though I walk through the valley of the shadow of death, I will fear no evil" (Ps. 23:4).
- "The Lord is my rock, my fortress, and my deliverer" (Ps. 18:2).

I remember when my daughter was four years old and she saw me laying my burdens at the cross one day as we were driving. She said, "Mommy, are you worrying about something?" I said, "No, baby. Mommy's giving her worries to God." This has opened up great discussion time with my kids.

Sometimes repeating Scripture to myself a few times is the right way; other times, depending on the worry at hand, I will need to draw on every truth I have hidden in my heart until that peace that passes all understanding comes in and overtakes my mind. You truly will not understand why you feel peace. You just will. It is supernatural!

You may not know it now, but that same power is alive in you and available to secure your victory if you are truly walking with the Lord. The Holy Spirit is able, equipped, and prepared to help you overcome anxiety and to give you the peace that passes all understanding. You may need to remind yourself over and over that your faith for victory is in the blood of Jesus. Jesus died so that you and I may have life and have it in abundance. He gave us His Word and sent us the Holy Spirit to be our helper.

Take the gift that God has for you. Meditate on and memorize the Word of God. You need to hide that Word in your heart so that when—not if!—fear and anxiety rear their ugly heads at you, you will be armed to fight in the name of Jesus and with the Word of God. After you have cast down that thought and called on the Word to proclaim the name of Jesus and refute the schemes of Satan, then you must keep proclaiming and meditating until you recognize that peace is covering you like a blanket.

Believe God Can Do It

Dear friend, if you are not strong enough in your faith to believe in the supernatural, you may struggle with realizing how serious God is about us avoiding idolatry and trusting only in Him. If your belief in God's ability to handle your anxiety isn't quite there, and you still find yourself turning to other defense mechanisms, I would suggest that you study the miracles Jesus did while He walked this earth. "Faith comes by hearing, and hearing by the Word of God" (Rom. 10:17, MEV). Our faith in God's ability to heal grows as we read how He has done it in the past.

You may need to read how Jesus turned water into wine, multiplied loaves and fish to feed thousands, healed the blind with spit and dirt, read people's minds, healed paralyzed individuals who hadn't walked in years, and raised people from the dead.

Right now, though, I want to give you a little miracles 101 lesson to increase your faith. I want to introduce you to one of my favorite people in the Bible: Joshua. We can learn a ton about God's miracle-working power by studying the Book of Joshua. Joshua was Moses's successor, and when Moses died, it was actually Joshua who led the Israelites into the Promised Land. Joshua had many battles to fight, but with God on his side he was guaranteed to win, and so are you.

In Joshua 6 we read about the fall of Jericho:

> Now the gates of Jericho were securely barred because of the Israelites. No one went out and no one came in.
>
> Then the Lord said to Joshua, "See, I have delivered Jericho into your hands, along with its king and its fighting men. March around the city once with all the armed men. Do this for six days. Have seven priests carry trumpets of rams' horns in front of the ark. On the seventh day, march around the city seven times, with the priests blowing the trumpets. When you hear them sound a loud blast on the trumpets, have the whole army give a loud shout;

> then the wall of the city will collapse and the army will go up, everyone straight in."
>
> —JOSHUA 6:1–5

Here we have the city of Jericho. This city was shut up tight. The people inside the city had heard about the Israelites and how they kept beating every army they came against. I am sure the people of Jericho thought, "Oh no, we are on lockdown." They shut every gate, and they shut every door. No one was getting in and no one out.

So God lets Joshua know, "No worries. You got this, and what you're going to do is march. You're going to march and blow trumpets. It's good old supernatural marching band time, my friend." God gives Joshua the plans and says in so many words, "We got this. I am handing them over to you. But you have to do exactly what I say."

Put yourself in Joshua's shoes. He's a warrior. Joshua is armed for battle. He knows he has to fight many battles to enter the Promised Land. But do you think Joshua thought he would be marching and blowing horns, much less trying to get soldiers excited about doing this? These are burly, manly men who left their wives and children to go to battle, and they are being told they are going to march behind the priests and blow horns.

What is Joshua having to depend on here? Faith! His faith in God's ability to deliver them is what gives God the green light to go. What if Joshua allowed fear of the unknown to come into play? What if Joshua decided: "*Well, God, that sounds nice and all, but I'm going with guns and knives*"? What if Joshua sold out? It would be idolatry, right? Joshua's faith is what moved God's hand, and that is exactly what will move God's hand where your anxiety is concerned. When you are tempted to sell out to idols that have let you down in the past, choose faith. Choose God's miracle-working power!

Let me tell you, while expecting a miracle from God, the first thing you need to know is that God decides when, God decides what, and God decides how. God uses methods we may never dream up in our wildest dreams when He does miracles. God's miracles are done God's way!

Well, then what happened?

> So Joshua son of Nun called the priests and said to them, "Take up the ark of the covenant of the LORD and have seven priests carry trumpets in front of it." And he ordered the army, "Advance! March around the city, with an armed guard going ahead of the ark of the LORD."
>
> When Joshua had spoken to the people, the seven priests carrying the seven trumpets before the LORD went forward, blowing their trumpets, and the ark of the LORD's covenant followed them. The armed guard marched ahead of the priests who blew the trumpets, and the rear guard followed the ark. All this time the trumpets were sounding. But Joshua had commanded the army, "Do not give a war cry, do not raise your voices, do not say a word until the day I tell you to shout. Then shout!" So he had the ark of the LORD carried around the city, circling it once. Then the army returned to camp and spent the night there.
>
> —JOSHUA 6:6–11

If you do not know what the ark of the Lord is, it is the wooden holder that was built to house the Law of Moses. It carried the Ten Commandments. This ark meant everything to the Israelites. It contained the laws God told Joshua to meditate on day and night and to never let this book of the law depart from their mouths, to be careful to do everything written in it.

The ark contained the laws that they were to follow. Old Testament law hinged on the fact that if you obeyed the law, you were blessed, and if you disobeyed the law, you were cursed. The old covenant was dependent solely on obedience, and because they were human like us, this law that was perfect demanded perfection, and they were unable to reach that perfect point, so God gave them all of the sacrifices that were necessary.

Praise God that today, because of Jesus, the perfect spotless Lamb, His sacrifice was enough, and it was the perfect sacrifice once for all for our sins! Jesus's sacrifice is why we no longer have to sacrifice rams and goats and other livestock over and over. Jesus died once for all of us.

This ark was everything to the Israelite people, and God's Word is everything to us today. Jesus is the Word made flesh. We love Jesus, and if we want to be like Jesus we have to learn His Word. If we want the miracle-working power available through God's Word, we have to read it, meditate on it, memorize it, bury it down in our hearts so deep no devil in hell could steal it from us. The Word and the Word made flesh, Jesus, are our lifeline in our fight against anxiety. We call on it. We confess it. We aim it at the enemy, and we trust it is enough, because it is.

Let's talk for a second about the priests who had to carry the ark. God instructed Joshua to have the priests march out front with the ark, and the people were to follow it. The soldiers were to march behind the guys with the robes.

Do you think that took some faith, my friend? I do. I would have wanted to march behind the guys who looked like football linebackers or bodyguards. But nope. They had to march behind the priests, the ones who had to keep their hands clean on a regular basis.

Today Jesus is the High Priest that we need to march behind day and night and never follow another, amen? As the writer of Hebrews says, "We do not have a high priest who is unable to empathize with our weaknesses, but we have one who has been tempted in every way, just as we are—yet he did not sin" (Heb. 4:15). We are no longer under the law as the Israelites were. Jesus fulfilled the law perfectly, and Jesus has become the guarantee of a better and new covenant.

Even so, we follow Jesus, our High Priest, like the Israelites followed the priests carrying the ark of the covenant marching around the walls of Jericho. In order for them to experience the supernatural work of God, they had to follow the ark, and we have to follow Jesus and His Word.

This leads me to my next point, which is that God's miracles follow His Word. God will never do miracles that don't line up with the Word. You see, whatever doesn't line up with the Word is usually disobedience, sin, or worldly pleasures. God does not use these things to bring His perfect will to pass or to perform miracles of any sort. Jesus is the Word made flesh. He is just like the Word, and the Word is just like Jesus. God doesn't go against His Son in doing miracles. God does miracles according to His Word. His Word goes before us all. With Jesus as our High Priest that we follow and the Word as our guide and our road map to life, we will see the miracle-working power of God in our mental healing.

Does the wall fall? Of course it does!

> On the seventh day, they got up at daybreak and marched around the city seven times in the same manner, except that on that day they circled the city seven times. The seventh time around, when the priests sounded the trumpet blast, Joshua commanded the army, "Shout! For the LORD has given you the city! The city and all that is in it are to be devoted to the LORD. Only Rahab the prostitute and all who are with her in her house shall be spared, because she hid the spies we sent. But keep away from the devoted things, so that you will not bring about your own destruction by taking any of them. Otherwise you will make the camp of Israel liable to destruction and bring trouble on it. All the silver and gold and the articles of bronze and iron are sacred to the LORD and must go into his treasury."
>
> When the trumpets sounded, the army shouted, and at the sound of the trumpet, when the men gave a loud shout, the walls collapsed; so everyone charged straight in, and they took the city.
>
> —JOSHUA 6:15–20

We can see here that God does miracles through people who believe that He will. Anxiety can control our thinking so drastically that it can interfere with our faith that God can do whatever He chooses to do. We may be frustrated because we are so fretful it's hard to concentrate. We may be starting to get mad that God hasn't miraculously just delivered us from it. We may even be ready to give up.

Dear friend, write this down. Tweet it, post it, do whatever you want with it, but please get it: Our faith moves God's hand. You have to believe God can heal you before

He will. You have to trust that when you put your cares at Jesus's feet at the cross, you are able to leave them there and not keep picking them back up again. He can handle them. You don't have to anymore. It's all about setting your faith to that and trusting. There is a supernatural law in effect where God's miracle-working power says, "Without faith, you will not see a miracle." The Word actually says, "Without faith it is impossible to please God" (Heb. 11:6). God is pleased with our faith, and He is pleased to do miracles for men and women and children of faith.

The key ingredient in God's miracles is faith. Jesus said this many times while He walked the earth healing people. "Your faith has healed you," He told them. God works miracles through people who believe He can do them.

For example:

- God used the disciples to heal people all through the Book of Acts because they realized they were filled with the Holy Spirit and that they had the power that came along with that privilege. That realization was their faith in action.
- God parted the Red Sea because Moses had the faith to put the stick in the water, believing God would part it.
- God stopped the Jordan River at flood stage for the Israelites to cross it because they had faith to put their foot in first and wait for God to stop it.

- God made the sun stand still for Joshua so the Israelites could win a battle in the daylight.

Again, God does miracles for people who have the faith to believe that He can. Do you believe God can heal you of your crippling anxiety? Do you believe He can set you free from your obsessive thoughts and behaviors that keep you bound in ways He never meant for you to experience? Do you believe He can make worry a thing of your past?

I will tell you, I have witnessed God do many miracles, including healing me of the torment of anxiety, not because I think God loves me any more than He loves anyone else. God is no respecter of persons. I believe God has allowed me to witness some supernatural experiences because He knows I have the faith of a child. I believe they are real—because they are.

The truth is, if your faith isn't where it needs to be, you will not trust in God to rescue you when you are in the middle of an anxiety attack or a distracting worry. He desires for us to call on Him and no one or nothing else for our strength to fight and win. It's time to put on our faith shoes. It's time to trust God in areas we have never trusted Him before. It's time to believe in miracles and watch God's peace that passes all understanding (Phil. 4:7) show up. It's time to go into battle like Joshua did and believe that what God said will come to pass will. Our peace will come. Our anxiety walls will fall. Our faith and trust in Him are the ammunition God will use to destroy it.

Remember, this will take time, but we have to start today. Our faith gets stronger every time we exercise it. Believe in the miracle-working power of God. This is not a get-well-quick remedy. You have to do your homework. You must invest your time and energy and determination. You have to practice casting down your anxious thoughts and replacing them with the Word until it becomes your new necessary habit. Then, before you know it, you will be so confident in who you are in Christ and the strength you have to defeat the devil that you will recognize peace as your daily companion.

Will you do it?

Standing With the Lord

As a new year approaches, so many of us automatically go to fresh starts, do overs, and renovating in our minds. We start thinking about what we want to accomplish this year on our own and as families. The Bible is jam packed with plan Bs and redos. I think that is my favorite thing about God. I mean, really, how many of us get everything right the first time? I would venture to say not many.

In the Book of Ezra we meet Ezra, a priest and an amazing leader. Ezra's humility and obedience to God helped lead the people of Israel back to the Lord. In the beginning of the book, we see God move in the heart of King Cyrus of Persia to rebuild the temple in Jerusalem that was destroyed under Nebuchadnezzar's reign. The people of Israel came back from exile, carrying their gifts into the treasury, ready for a fresh start for God's people. The people assembled and began building, when of course they came up against opposition. That's no surprise, right? I love when Paul says in the first letter to the Corinthians, "A great door for effective work has opened to me, and there are many who oppose me" (1 Cor. 16:9).

Every time we are dedicated to doing something God is calling us to do, you better believe the world will throw some fiery darts our way to try to get us out of the race. But fear not. We have Jesus! We are destined to triumph when we fight with Him. Jesus says, "In this world you will have trouble. But take heart! I have overcome the world" (John 16:33).

So the people had to halt building because of a few onlookers who decided to write a letter to the kingdom trying to get the king in fear that if the people of Jerusalem built this temple, they would fail to pay taxes to the kingdom. Well, nothing speaks volumes to insecure authority like dollar bills. So, the king sent a decree to halt the building of the temple. The work on the temple stopped until the second year of the reign of the next king, King Darius of Persia.

Everything changed when a few very smart servants of the Lord approached the king and asked him to search the archives to find that King Cyrus originally issued a decree to rebuild the temple. If something was decreed by the king, it was law. So King Darius found the decree and allowed the people of Jerusalem to return to building.

Before they knew it, the temple was rebuilt, and God's people were celebrating the dedication of the house of God with joy—until the priest Ezra returned to Jerusalem from exile eighty years later and found that God's people (including the priests) had intermarried with people and were practicing pagan rituals and worshipping idols. Ezra was appalled at the lack of faithfulness of the Israelites, and he demanded that God's people unyoke themselves from people worshipping other gods. Ezra's conviction and confession before God for Israel's sin became contagious, and the people of Israel returned to the Lord again in repentance.

I was immediately convicted reading this. I questioned myself, saying, "Do you stand up for the things of God even if it means people may follow you or may not? Do you care more about standing righteous in front of God or blending in with friends and acquaintances? Are you sold out for God's ideas of right or wrong, or are you tempted to sometimes intermarry with the world?"

I realized that once again God was pressing on my people-pleasing scar. Ezra could have returned and worshipped the Lord how he deemed right and ignored the sins of those around him. But he didn't. He called those around him to stand up for what was right alongside him. And in return, God allowed him to pen what scholars believe to be most of 1 and 2 Chronicles, Ezra, Nehemiah, and Psalm 119. God gave Ezra a few chapters in His love letter to us, an honor that sold-out people pleasers will never experience.

I'm sure it wasn't an easy road to walk. But usually those paths that lead straight heavenward aren't.

http://momydlo.wordpress.com
/2013/12/30/standing-with-the-lord

HOMEWORK

Spend time in prayer as you answer the following questions.

1. *Where have you made for yourself any idols?*

2. *What kind of radical moves for Jesus can you make to cast down these idols?*

3. *How much of God's Word is hidden in your heart to battle anxiety victoriously?*

4. *What kind of plan can you make to begin hiding more of God's Word in your heart?*

5. Do you believe in miracles?

6. Tell of a time where you experienced the supernatural power of God working miracles in your life.

Read the following scriptures and rewrite them in your own words:

- Exodus 20:4
- Philippians 3:7
- Philippians 4:4–8

- 2 Corinthians 10:5

- Psalm 119:11

Memorize

> Do not be anxious about anything, but in every situation, by prayer and petition, with thanksgiving, present your requests to God. And the peace of God, which transcends all understanding, will guard your hearts and minds in Christ Jesus.
>
> —Philippians 4:6–7

Confession

Practice saying out loud over and over this week: "I cast all my cares on the Lord. This too shall pass."

Application

Work on immediately casting down imaginations and replacing them with God's Word.

Journal Time

This week, each day that you journal, write down at least ten things you are thankful for.

Chapter 3

CONFIDENCE IN CHRIST

Fears and anxieties can be so compartmentalized, it can make it hard for people to explain to others what they are dealing with because they are usually a little scared that no one else struggles with those same weird thoughts. The truth is, we all struggle with thoughts that pop into our minds that we wish we never experienced. But we need to know that those thoughts are not sin. Rather, they are a *temptation* to sin. It is up to us to practice self-control and avoid acting on those temptations. It is up to us to cast down evil thoughts or intentions and replace them with the truths in God's Word.

Yes, people worry about different things. Our different talents, abilities, and strengths as well as our weaknesses, struggles, and challenges affect what causes us to be insecure or fear a situation. Throughout my years of researching anxiety, this has struck me as so interesting, the realization that some things can bug some people when others have no issue with it at all, but those other people have their own struggles.

I have met many people, for example, who have obsessive fears of physical sickness or disease while other people put little thought toward it. Some people have fears of financial ruin or lack while other people seem to trust in

God's provision no matter what their bank accounts look like. There are people who worry about what people think about them while other people are not affected by others' opinions all that much. Things as silly as hearing someone has the stomach flu or head lice can immediately trigger anxiety in some people, but others can brush these conditions off as simple distractions or annoyances in life.

When people share their struggles, you can almost see the "please don't think I'm crazy" look on their faces. The truth is, until they put their thoughts out there, the enemy wins the battle by getting them to keep quiet. But once those thoughts are released, the strength of the fear is broken. That is the beauty of confessing our struggles and sins to God and then to someone we trust deeply. This transparency and vulnerability is healing on so many levels.

I have been called by God to be completely authentic about what I struggle with. God has actually said, "Mo, you have to be real so people can get healed." So I will confess one of my real struggles to you. I struggle still today with one main anxiety, and it's a big one: my unrealistic desire to control! When I say control, I mean my nature wants to control everything around me.

I want to control things, people, inanimate objects such as the weather, and people's personalities. I want to control how people feel about me, what they say to me, and how they act around me. I want to protect people from being hurt. I want to help those who are hurting. I want healing for anyone sick. I want to see every soul saved and promised heaven someday. I am burdened minute by minute with a desire to fix whatever is wrong with whomever I come in contact with. I want to help those who struggle with addictions to be set free. I want to see unkind people treat people better. I want to help my son who is struggling with reading just to all of a sudden get it. I want to pick godly spouses for my kids and then just say, "OK, here she is." I want to look into the future to see that my husband will always choose me and not trade me in for a younger version when I start looking my age. I want to never be interrupted again when I am in the middle of a good thought and trying to get it down on paper. I want to be 100 percent assured that no one will ever hurt my children or nieces or nephews. I want to snap my fingers so that my children all of a sudden like vegetables. I want to get my dog to stop digging holes and dragging in the dirt.

May I just say something in plain terms? I am a hot mess when I'm too far from Jesus. Yet for some reason, God seems pretty in love with me. I think it may be fun for Him to teach me over and over, "Mo, I'm God. You are not." When I learn that perpetual lesson and I submit to His leadership, I think I mature a little bit more. And even better than that, I think I fall more in love with Him too.

But let me tell you this. It has not always been easy standing on a pulpit and saying, "I'm a hot mess. Can I share the gospel with you?" I kept my guard up for so long because the enemy had me believing people would question my leadership abilities if they knew I didn't have it all together. I was even taught this by my spiritual mentors a couple times—until the Holy Spirit got ahold of me and said, "Mo, you are Mine. Tell the world you struggle when you get your eyes off of Me."

So I'll be quite honest with you. I can't even get a millimeter away from my great counselor. The Holy Spirit reigns supreme in my life, and I take absolutely no credit for anything I have done to overcome anxiety and mental attack. But if I was going to boast, it would be about what the Holy Spirit and God's Word has done with a hot mess like me who just never gives up fighting.

Where's Your Confidence?

In 2 Corinthians 11 the Apostle Paul was at this same point, in my opinion. He was a little fed up with the Corinthian church and was giving them a piece of his mind because he saw them so easily swayed by wrong doctrine. Then he started defending himself. However, realizing they might think he was being boastful, he says in 2 Corinthians 11:30, "If I must boast, I will boast of the things that show my weakness." We find out later in his little spiritual rant why he was boasting in his weakness, where he speaks the popular scripture that says, "But he said to me, 'My grace is sufficient for you, for my power is made perfect in weakness.' Therefore I will boast all the more gladly about my weaknesses, so that Christ's power may rest on me. That is why, for Christ's sake, I delight in weaknesses, in insults, in hardships, in persecutions, in difficulties. For when I am weak, then I am strong" (2 Cor. 12:9–10).

This scripture helped me realize that if the Apostle Paul felt as if he had to be transparent to get souls to submit to the Savior, then of course transparency needs to be my ministry strategy as well. Paul described the Lord's strength in his life showing up when he was at his weakest. So when I stand on the pulpit and bare my soul to the level of "Please, Lord, hold me up and help me get this out," I am confident that the Lord will show up on my behalf, and He always has.

Here's the truth: our weakness is where the grace of God can flow the strongest. Paul's thorn in the flesh that he speaks about is once again related to that God-shaped hole in our lives. For many of us, these God-shaped holes are our mental strongholds that need to be broken—and can be, if we submit to God's leadership. God's grace helps us get our minds off our sin and on our righteousness. We need to tell ourselves over and over until we believe it, "I am the righteousness of God in Christ Jesus." You are righteous only because of, always because of, and forever because of our High Priest, Jesus.

So we need to get a little grace-minded. We need to get a little excited about what grace means. Grace means we have the power to fight habits, strongholds, sickness, disease, poverty, depression, anxiety, and worry. Don't those struggles make you feel weak? Well, remember what Paul says about that in 2 Corinthians 12? God tells him, "My grace is sufficient for you. My power is made perfect in weakness." When we are weak, we are strong! Yes, because when we are weak, grace shows up.

Let me tell you something I have noticed about God. He is very close to the brokenhearted. When you are going through something so hard, sometimes it is amazing the supernatural peace you have going through it. In the natural that situation would literally bring you to your knees and cause you to quit, but because of the grace of God you are able to persevere. That's God's grace!

God's grace is sufficient for us when we are struggling. When we stay occupied with Jesus and with His righteousness, provision, protection, and strength, then we are strong. Do you have confidence in this?

Confidence in God's Leadership

Our confidence in God takes many shapes, and the first area where we must develop that confidence is in God's leadership. We must trust the leadership of the Holy Spirit in order to break free in our thinking.

Here's one way that works. Psalm 23 speaks of God as our shepherd, and in verse 2 we read that He leads us beside quiet waters. That phrase *quiet waters* speaks peace to me. You want to know why? Because I have a screened-in porch on the back of my house with a tin roof. Ever heard the rain on a tin roof? You could be sitting having a quiet conversation with someone on the porch, and then once that rain hits, you find yourself almost yelling just to hear each other. Sometimes that white noise can be like a box fan whipping in your ear or the sound of an engine on a 747 taking off right outside your window. It is painfully loud.

But God leads us near quiet waters. His leadership is like that. And these quiet waters are like the sound of a pond in a valley where you can hear bullfrogs and crickets and the whipping of dragonfly wings. The world leads us to tin roofs in a rainstorm, but God leads us to still waters. Don't you want to trust that kind of leadership? I hope so, because let me tell you this: our leader can be trusted.

We have to be confident in God's leadership ability, but quite honestly, submitting to leadership is tough for many of us control freaks. Am I right? Well, control freaks such as me and the Apostle Paul have learned the hard way to put our confidence in God's leadership abilities. For example, in Acts 16 Paul and his companions show perfect submission to the leadership of the Holy Spirit:

> Paul and his companions traveled throughout the region of Phrygia and Galatia, having been kept by the Holy Spirit from preaching the word in the province of Asia. When they came to the border of Mysia, they tried to enter Bithynia, but the Spirit of Jesus would not allow them to. So they passed by Mysia and went down to Troas. During the night Paul had a vision of a man of Macedonia standing and begging him, "Come over to Macedonia and help us." After Paul had seen the vision, we got ready at once to leave for Macedonia, concluding that God had called us to preach the gospel to them.
>
> —Acts 16:6–10

Our good sense as Christians tends to make us think the gospel needs to be preached everywhere. So why would the Holy Spirit not allow Paul and his companions to go into these towns? I don't know. But God does. The Holy Spirit could have been protecting them from danger or keeping them from wasting time if the people were hard-hearted toward the message. Simply put, their plan wasn't God's plan, and God had to straighten them out.

Oh, I have been there so many times! I have felt the urge to help someone or fill a volunteer need that was presented in front of me but the Holy Spirit would just nudge me to keep my mouth closed and be still. I had no idea why. But God did. I trust His leadership—period!

Let me share with you a story of how God is continuing to teach me to place my confidence in His leadership. The first day of school this year was wonderful. My kiddos all got out the door on time, looking like a million bucks, all prepared for the new school year with their squeaking new sneakers and their crisply starched backpacks. I was so excited to sit down at the computer and begin to write what I thought was going to be the message I would preach at my next event. Seriously, working as a writer from home in the summer with four kids in and out of the house is kind of comical. It just isn't going to happen. So I had some catching up to do.

Then I realized my Wi-Fi wasn't working. Well, I couldn't even call my husband to tell him of my dilemma because I also had no phone. Two days earlier my sixteen-year-old daughter had suffered a cell phone tragedy when one of her trophies fell off her shelf and shattered her brand-new phone. A sixteen-year-old without a cell phone in her hand feels as if she has just suffered an amputation. So I let her borrow my phone while hers was being fixed.

At this point, with no phone and no computer, I borrowed my son's phone to tell Tommy about our Wi-Fi when I realized it was all of our cable—our TV as well. Oh, and I forgot to mention that my husband had just turned in his company car when he switched jobs, so he also had my car that day. No phone, no computer, no TV, and no car. I thought to myself, "OK, Lord, I get it. I still have a Bible, though, right?" So I went outside to study.

Here's the gospel truth. Within about fifteen minutes of having my Bible open and my mouth shut, inside a house that sounded like still waters instead of a tin roof in a rainstorm, I had a completely mapped out message that was totally different than what I had planned to write. And there is more! After I had studied and mapped out my message, I was enjoying a quiet home, praying and doing some light housework, when I started to get a little chilly in the air-conditioning so I decided to walk out back to warm up a bit. I walked out back and noticed some balls on the lawn, so I picked them up. Then I made my way to the front of the house, grabbed the mail, and brought in the garbage cans. It was then I heard the quiet prompting of the Holy Spirit say to me, "Check Trav's oil."

Travis is my brand-new college student. He lives at home and attends the community college in town. Travis and a friend were in his room hanging out, and I walked in and said, "Trav, pull your car in the garage. Let's check your oil." I had been asking my husband to show Travis how to check the oil in his car, but my husband had been busy with his new position at work and hadn't had a chance. I thought I'd better show him myself.

We popped the hood and got out the manual to find the dipstick, and I grabbed a rag to show my son and his friend how to check the oil. To my surprise, it was bone dry! I couldn't find a smudge of oil on the rag. My heart was racing, and all I could think was, "Another one bites the dust." I adore my sweet husband, but he can blow an engine on a cash car quicker than you can say Jiffy Lube! I calmed my nerves and told Travis and his friend to get in the car, that we were going to pray that it got us one mile down the road to the auto parts store to buy oil.

Once we got there, I had the technician come out and check it as well, then show the boys the proper way to put the oil in and explain the importance of oil in a car. We then got back on the road, driving extremely quiet, as I think we all were thinking about our obvious blessing of God.

What if my TV had been working? What if I went and wrote the original message I had an idea to write? What if my daughter's phone didn't break and I'd been distracted by social media on my phone? I wouldn't have heard God say, "Check Trav's oil." Then Travis would have been out of a vehicle to drive to college and work, and that group for my booked event would have received a word from Mo instead of a word from the Lord. (Please know, a word from Mo stinks!)

I told you I boast in my sufferings and weaknesses because then Christ's power comes through. When I am weak, God is strong. I can't write a lick without the prompting of the Holy Spirit. You might buy one of my books written that way, but you wouldn't buy a second. God stripped me of a phone, a TV, a computer, and a car that day to speak to me so I would listen—so I would trust only His leadership and guidance. What else are we missing that God is trying to tell us because we won't unplug long enough to hear?

All that to say, I put my confidence in God's leadership abilities. When God says, "Go for a walk," I go for a walk. When God says, "Don't eat that!" I don't eat it. When God says, "Time to go to the doctor," I go to the doctor. I try my hardest to submit to God's leadership. But if I can't hear Him, I am leading myself, and that is dangerous ground. We need to be confident in Christ's leadership. He truly leads us beside still waters.

Confidence in Christ's Sufficiency

We also must be confident in God's sufficiency. He is enough! If you have God and nothing else, you have everything. If God be for us, who can be against us? I love Hebrews 10:32–35, where it reads:

> Remember those earlier days after you had received the light, when you endured in a great conflict full of suffering. Sometimes you were publicly exposed

> to insult and persecution; at other times you stood side by side with those who were so treated. You suffered along with those in prison and joyfully accepted the confiscation of your property, because you knew that you yourselves had better and lasting possessions. So do not throw away your confidence; it will be richly rewarded.

These disciples had experienced the real deal in Jesus and then the real deal in being filled with the power of the Holy Spirit, and they decided it was sufficient. Jesus was enough. Being saved and being used by God was enough. And the Word goes right into confidence after that. The sufficiency of Christ gave them confidence—confidence in Christ's ability made manifest in them.

We have to remember where our true help comes from. Our help doesn't come from Jesus and the security system. Our true help does not come from Jesus and our gun. Our true help does not come from Jesus and our cell phone. Jesus is all we need. My phone did not tell me to check Travis's oil. My TV did not tell me to check Travis's oil. My computer did not tell me to check Travis's oil. The Holy Spirit living on the inside of me told me to check his oil. His grace is sufficient for me. His power was made perfect in my life that day because I felt somewhat weak without some of my other defense mechanisms around.

Ever turned the car around to head home to grab your cell phone because you were afraid to be without it? Ever turned on the TV in the house just to have some noise because the second the quiet happens, you are fighting voices? Ever go on social media to comment on things that really aren't your business at all because it made you feel less lonely? I understand. I have too. But the truth is that when we do these things, we throw away our confidence in what Christ alone can do in our lives. Isaiah 30:15 says, "In repentance and rest is your salvation, in quietness and trust is your strength." We are strengthened by trusting in God's sufficiency. Not God and the phone. Not God and the TV. Not God and medication. Not God and an insurance policy. Christ is sufficient!

Isaiah 26:3–4 says, "You will keep in perfect peace those whose minds are steadfast, because they trust in you. Trust in the LORD forever, for the LORD, the LORD himself, is the Rock eternal." Do you want perfect peace? I know I do. You can't buy peace. You can't manufacture peace. You can't produce peace. True and lasting peace comes only from a personal love relationship with Jesus Christ and renewing our minds by keeping our minds steadfast on Him.

We do not need to add anything to God's equation for our lives. It is God + nothing = everything! As Ephesians 3:12 says, "In him and through faith in him we may approach God with freedom and confidence." We must be confident in God's leadership. We must be confident in God's sufficiency. And we must be confident in God's protection—which brings me to the next point.

Confidence in God's Protection

All of Psalm 91 speaks of God's protection for those who acknowledge His name. Verse 14 tells us the Lord says, "Because he loves me...I will rescue him; I will protect him, for he acknowledges my name." God promises to protect us, and I have confidence in His protection. When I take my eyes off of this promise, fear attempts to creep in. But as soon as I renew my mind to this truth, I return to His perfect peace.

You see, there truly is nothing to fear when you are in the arms of the Lord. When faced with the "My daddy is stronger than your daddy" argument, Christians win every time. I know this because it's scriptural. First John 4:4 says, "You, dear children, are from God and have overcome them, because the one who is in you is greater than the one who is in the world." There you have it. The Holy Spirit inside you can't lose.

Did I say you wouldn't fight or struggle or face an adversary? No! Paul testified, "Because a great door for effective work has opened to me, and there are many who oppose me" (1 Cor. 16:9). Anytime you attempt to do something great for God, plan on opposition from the enemy. But you cannot fear it. That is the key. We fight the fear of facing the devil at every turn by putting our confidence in God's protection. He fights for His children. That's the simple truth. And, my friend, if God is fighting for you, you are guaranteed victory. It may not seem like victory all of the time. But God doesn't give His glory to anyone else. I promise you that.

In the Book of Acts one of the teachers of the law named Gamaliel says it perfectly as he encourages the Sanhedrin to leave the apostles alone. He says, "For if their purpose or activity is of human origin, it will fail. But if it is from God, you will not be able to stop these men; you will only find yourself fighting against God" (Acts 5:38–39).

We need to put our confidence in God's protection of us. He has given us every tool we need to fight. We have the Holy Spirit, the Word of God, the blood of Jesus shed for us, the power of the name of Jesus to break strongholds and cause demons to flee, and the covering of the Father as He shadows us with His wings. We must simply dwell in that shadow of the Almighty and never stray.

What does God want from us in order to offer us this protection? Remember what Psalm 91:14 says: "Because He loves me...I will rescue him." He simply wants our love. He adores us. He is enamored with us. We cannot fathom in our most supernatural of days a tiny glimpse of the amount of love God has for us. All He asks is that we love Him in return, and then He offers us His protection. Pretty nice deal, am I right? To love and be loved by the maker of the universe? And with that love, we are promised His protection. I say yes to that! I need His protection. It is my peace.

Confidence in the Name of Jesus

It seems as if whenever I am finishing up a book or writing a message or helping someone on a substantial level, I face opposition. I have seen demons in my dreams and in my bedroom. They have shaken the pot rack in my kitchen while I was writing, and they have caused my computer to freeze up more times than once the second I am writing about their attacks.

For the longest time, my husband, Tommy, had never personally felt the presence of a demon in our midst, but there had been countless times he had woken me from a sound sleep because I was yelling, "Satan, get away in the name of Jesus!" But then the other night, he saw one. We had gone to bed exhausted from serving the Lord all day at a mission project. We began to have a disagreement about something, and we tried to go to bed without resolving it.

Well, there is a reason why the Word says, "Do not let the sun go down while you are still angry, and do not give the devil a foothold" (Eph. 4:26–27). Within a few minutes of trying to go to sleep, Tommy reached over to me and said, "Mo, I'm so sorry you deal with this all the time. I just saw a demon in our room. I had to cast it out in Jesus's name."

I rolled over and hugged him and realized that our argument was playing right into Satan's plan. His demons were right there, working to cause division between us. Tommy cast them out in Jesus's name, and then we apologized to each other to overcome evil with love, as the Bible teaches us to do.

Because the truth in all of this is that we fight demons. We don't want to think about the fact that there is a spiritual battle going on and that we are in a battle—and we aren't in battle with mere soldiers. We fight principalities and evil forces in heavenly realms! Satan and his demons absolutely hate the gospel preached, souls being saved, and people growing in Christ, so these demons work extra hard to fight us on a daily basis. Satan throws fiery darts of offense, temptation, and lies our way minute by minute to counteract God's perfect will for our lives. But we must not fear his manipulation. We are more than conquerors in Christ Jesus, and we draw our strength by putting our confidence in God's protection of us and in the power of Jesus's name.

We must fight confidently with the Word of God, with prayer, and with truth affirmations, but most of all with the name of Jesus, because at the name of Jesus, demons have to flee. They have no choice. They have no power over the name of Jesus. The name of Jesus needs to be on our tongues anytime we are attacked by the enemy and his demons.

As long as you walk this earth and profess Jesus Christ as your Lord and Savior and do anything to share that faith with others, you will have to know how to fight. But there is no doubt you are guaranteed to win with Jesus as your protector. (In the next couple chapters we will discuss strategies to fight and win against the enemy of your soul.) Satan desires to steal your peace, but you have the authority in Christ Jesus to overcome the schemes of the devil once and for all. The grace of God is our protection, and that grace flows in our lives because of what Jesus did on the cross. We are saved by grace through faith in Christ.

When grace shows up,
We can say no to sin.

When grace shows up,
We can conquer the enemy's attacks.

When grace shows up,
We can put the past to death once and for all.

When grace shows up,
We can get excited about our future in Christ.

When grace shows up,
People can get saved.

When grace shows up,
We are free to love.

We have to trust in God's protection that He has for us. You see, I don't fear being alone. I don't fear the attack of the enemy. I don't fear demons. That's because I know who I am in Christ. I am a co-heir with Jesus, a daughter of the King of kings. I have been adopted into God's family. I dine at His table. I don't eat off the floor with the dogs. I am more than a conqueror, righteous and ready for the battle. I simply have to have the name of Jesus in my holster, and I have everything I need.

We must remember who we are and whose we are! We belong to God. He will not let the righteous fall, and we are righteous because of what our Lord Jesus Christ did for us on Calvary's cross. We cannot become righteous or earn righteousness. Our right standing with God is determined by our faith in His Son.

We must put our confidence in God's leadership. We must put our confidence in God's sufficiency. We must put our confidence in God's protection. And we must put our confidence in the name of Jesus, which holds power in and of itself.

Since the Holy Spirit is exactly like Jesus Christ and since we are filled with the Holy Spirit, we have everything we need for godliness and holy living at our fingertips. Remember what we learned from Paul. It is OK to be weak, because where we are weak, God releases more of His grace to flow. So when we are weak, we are actually strong! He then is able to lead. He then is able to protect. He then is all we need. Let's get ourselves out of the way and put our confidence in Christ.

What If You Were Moses?

This morning I was reading in Exodus where God speaks to Moses in the burning bush. Wow, I love the Word, because God gave me a fresh revelation this morning on a passage I have read many times. He showed me how many times Moses asked God, "What if?" When God says in so many words that Moses is going to lead His people into the land of milk and honey and out of slavery, Moses wants confirmation after confirmation.

First Moses asks, "Who do I tell them talked to me and told me this?" God says, "Tell them I Am sent you." Then Moses asks, "What if they don't believe me or listen?" Then God has him set down his staff, turns it into a snake, then has him pick it back up, and it's a staff again. That one would have been enough for me. After all, at this point he's talking to a burning bush with a voice, right? But the staff isn't enough for Moses. God knows it, so He has to show Moses how He can turn his hand leprous and then heal it once Moses sticks it in his cloak. I'm thinking, "OK, enough already. He's God! Tell the people they are going to be free, and call it a day, Moses!"

Yet Moses has a few more reasons to tell God He may have made a mistake in picking him. He says, "Lord, I have never been eloquent." Pretty much, he's telling God, "Lord, I am not your average Billy Graham. Are you sure there isn't anyone else You can visit in a bush?" But God so lovingly and patiently asks, "Who gave man this mouth?

Who makes him deaf or mute? Is it not I, the Lord? Now go, I will help you speak and teach you what to say."

I was feeling for Moses at this point because I have been there. When I hear way too many times that God wants women to be quiet in church but then God calls me to teach the Word, I am forced to ask, "Lord, are You sure You mean me? Remember, I am a woman." But I think this ticks God off a little. God is like, "Really, Mo? I think I know you are a woman. I made you!"

So here is where I relate more to God than Moses. Moses whines one more time. He flat out asks God to send someone else. And the Word says God's anger burned against Moses. But God kindly decides to give Moses the help of his brother Aaron to ease his worries anyway. And thank You, Jesus, that God does that for us sometimes too.

Seriously, when God called me to start Unforsaken Ministries, I'm so grateful He knew I was still a little too insecure to not have a sister or two by my side. My friend Jean and my friend Dana have been next to me, step by step. My friends Crystal and Pam have encouraged me, insecure moment by insecure moment. Was God enough for me? Oh, heck yes, but He was also loving enough to know I needed a couple girlfriends to ease the burden a little.

So yes, Moses was a little thickheaded. Aren't we all? Has God specifically called you to do something but the voices of man ring over and over in your heart so you need God to confirm it four times when once should have been enough? Do you have a calling you are hoping God will just hand to someone more eloquent? Are you afraid people won't believe you are the real deal?

I want to encourage you today to take God at His first word. He is a sure thing. He doesn't leave us alone to venture into new territory by ourselves. We are unforsaken! He strengthens us as we take each step, knowing that His feet have already paved the way. He goes before us, and He is our rear guard. Trust Him today. God already knows your weaknesses. Don't remind Him of them. He made you!

http://momydlo.wordpress.com
/2014/03/11/what-if-you-were-moses

Homework

Spend some time in prayer as you answer the following questions.

1. *When have you recognized God's grace covering you in a tough situation?*

2. When have you noticed God leading you beside still waters?

3. What things or people do you sometimes place your confidence in, besides Christ?

4. How do you trust in God's protection of you and your family?

5. What is it like for you to consider that you have everything you need on the inside of you to fight the devil and win?

Read the following scriptures and rewrite them in your own words:

- Hebrews 3:13–15

- Hebrews 10:19
- Hebrews 10:35
- Psalm 91:14–16
- Romans 8:14–15
- Philippians 1:5–6
- Philippians 4:12–13

MEMORIZE

> But he said to me, "My grace is sufficient for you, for my power is made perfect in weakness."
>
> —2 CORINTHIANS 12:9

CONFESSION

Practice saying out loud over and over this week: "All I need is Jesus. If God be for me, who could be against me?"

APPLICATION

Work on turning off the distractions in your home more often this week, such as your phone, TV, or computer so that you can find the quiet time needed to hear correctly from God.

Journal Time

Take some time to let God know where you have had fear lately. Cast your fears on Him and watch His perfect love cast out your fear. Be honest, transparent, and real.

Chapter 4

A LOOK AT SPIRITUAL WARFARE

I WANT TO START by asking one question: What is up with 3:00 a.m.? Do you have a hard time embracing the 3:00 a.m. struggle too? I don't know what is going on in the spiritual world at that hour, but 3:00 a.m. never feels lovely to me. Here comes the voices: "*Oh Mo, you didn't handle that well with your son today. You don't have any patience. What if you didn't have your kids anymore? Then you would be sorry. You are a terrible mother. Most mothers would have spent more time asking him how he felt, you just jumped in and gave your opinion. Oh, all of your opinions, people are so sick of them. You think they are listening to your teaching? Your best friends don't even come to hear you teach. You are so wrong. You aren't a Bible teacher. God never called you. You've made this one up in your head.*" And on and on it goes. Three o'clock in the morning always seems to be the time the spirit of fear and anxious thinking presents itself.

One time my husband went away for business for five days, and I swear Satan was even messing with my dog at 3:00 a.m. She woke up and whined each night at that time. I know it was just the devil trying to torment me and steal my peace, but as much as I hated getting out of bed to let the dog out and then back in, I was able to practice some of my techniques for resting in God, trusting and meditating on the Word of God until I could return to sleep.

But it makes sense this would happen. Do you know Satan works overtime at night? Even Jesus talks about this. He says, "Are there not twelve hours of daylight? Anyone who walks in the daytime will not stumble, for they see by the world's light. It is when a person walks at night that they stumble, for they have no light" (John 11:9–10).

Friend, I know a lot of us struggle like crazy at night. Please know this is very normal and to be expected. That is why God put several scriptures in His Word concerning the night and sleep. I am going to share a few of them with you right now. Meditate on these today, so that you can be armed and ready to fight the next time Satan attacks:

- "In peace I will lie down and sleep, for you alone, LORD, make me dwell in safety" (Ps. 4:8).
- "He will not let your foot slip—he who watches over you will not slumber; indeed, he who watches over Israel will neither slumber nor sleep" (Ps. 121:3–4).
- "Unless the LORD builds the house, the builders labor in vain. Unless the LORD watches over the city, the guards stand watch in vain" (Ps. 127:1).

It's an All-Out War

So let's dive into the reality that you're in the middle of a war. You are in the dead center of two opposing forces trying to take control over some cherished land—you!

By way of example, let me tell you about the very vivid dream I had that I believe was a vision from God. In the dream I was playing piano and the most beautiful classical music was coming from my fingertips. I was saying in the dream, "God is doing it! I don't know how to play piano on my own. I just keep moving my fingers." In the dream people kept putting me in front of pianos. When they couldn't find one, they handed me little keyboards, and the same beautiful music kept playing.

Then all of a sudden the pianos were gone, and sharp knives were being hurled at me from every direction. Amazingly I was able to catch the handle of every knife in my hands before it could touch me. Through it all I had no fear. In the morning I awoke to do my Bible study and knew God had shown me a lesson about trusting Him completely and watching beauty flow from that trust. The knives were nothing but the devil's attempt to steal what God was trying to do. But you see, I had no fear, so Satan had no victory!

Then in Philippians 1:27–28 I read, "Whatever happens, conduct yourselves in a manner worthy of the gospel of Christ. Then, whether I come and see you or only hear about you in my absence, I will know that you stand firm in the one Spirit, striving together as one for the faith of the gospel without being frightened in any way by those who oppose you. This is a sign to them that they will be destroyed, but that you will be saved—and that by God."

I believe God showed me through all this that to live without bowing down to the fear that Satan wants us to feel and feeling peace instead is not only a gift that God has for us, it is also a sign to others about our salvation. Our courage leads others to Jesus. When we can beat the devil at his own game like contenders in a boxing match by not fearing the knives that he aims at us, God is able to do supernatural things through us.

A War of Two Natures

A reality of this war is demonstrated through the story of Jacob and Esau, told in Genesis 25:21–34:

> Isaac prayed to the LORD on behalf of his wife, because she was childless. The LORD answered his prayer, and his wife Rebekah became pregnant. The babies jostled each other within her, and she said, "Why is this happening to me?" So she went to inquire of the LORD.
>
> The LORD said to her,
>
> "Two nations are within your womb,
> and two peoples from within you will be separated;
> one people will be stronger than the other,
> and the older will serve the younger."
>
> When the time came for her to give birth, there were twin boys in her womb. The first to come out was red, and his whole body was like a hairy garment; so they named him Esau. After this, his brother came out, with his hand grasping Esau's heel; so he was named Jacob. Isaac was sixty years old when Rebekah gave birth to them.
>
> The boys grew up, and Esau became a skillful hunter, a man of the open country, while Jacob was content to stay at home among the tents. Isaac, who had a taste for wild game, loved Esau, but Rebekah loved Jacob.

> Once when Jacob was cooking some stew, Esau came in from the open country, famished. He said to Jacob, "Quick, let me have some of that red stew! I'm famished!" (That was why he was also called Edom.)
>
> Jacob replied, "First, sell me your birthright."
>
> "Look, I am about to die," Esau said. "What good is the birthright to me?"
>
> But Jacob said, "Swear to me first." So he swore an oath to him, selling his birthright to Jacob.
>
> Then Jacob gave Esau some bread and some lentil stew. He ate and drank, and then got up and left.
>
> So Esau despised his birthright.

Let's look specifically at verse 23 and what the Lord says about the two brothers: "Two nations are in your womb, and two peoples from within you will be separated; one people will be stronger than the other, and the older will serve the younger." We have two nations in our wombs, ladies. We are born of the flesh. Our flesh is sinful. It is eager to get its own way, and our flesh wants to gratify its evil desires. That is represented by Esau. Esau had his inheritance at stake, and he sold it for some soup. (Come on, really? Not even chocolate?) Jacob had enough sense to realize that he could endure some hunger pains and maybe even feel sick to his stomach for a little while in order to get the lasting benefits of being called the firstborn.

When you became born again and gave your life to Christ, you became filled with the Holy Spirit. This means you are joint heirs with Christ, and you now have full dominion over the devil's schemes and your own flesh. You have the power on the inside of you to fight any temptation that comes your way. You have the name of Jesus to call upon, and God's Word says, "And these signs will accompany those who believe: In my name they will drive out demons" (Mark 16:17).

You have the authority to call on Jesus at any time, day or night, whether you feel powerful or not. You can call on the name of Jesus and be saved. Not just saved for your eternal salvation, but also saved from temptation.

My friend, anxiety is a form of temptation that Satan uses against you. He wants you to feel as if you have ultimate control over your life. When we are truly following Christ, though, we know that God is in control. Satan wants to steal that from God however he can, and if that means getting you to believe you have to control situations by tormenting you with anxiety, then he will gladly do it. Anxiety is really an illusion of control. Worrying about something, fretting about something, and dwelling on it over and over in our heads binds us and tricks us into believing we are solving the issue. When really it is just paralyzing us. It's a tool of the enemy. He will try to get you to give up your birthright for a bowl of soup. Don't give him that satisfaction.

God says to Rebekah, "The older will serve the younger." The truth is, your old flesh must serve the new Spirit inside you. It has to bow down. Remember your birthright! We have to renew our minds and know that we have the power inside us to battle and win. Just as Jacob had the strength to give up or fast from the soup, you can fast from worry.

Right here and now I want to encourage you to go on a fast from worrying. Each time the devil rears his ugly head with fear, say out loud, "No! I am fasting anxiety. No fear here!" Make a commitment to fast from poor thinking. Start with one day. When you realize you went one full day without worrying, then you can make it a two-day fast. When you can go two straight days without fear or anxiety, you will be amazed at how proud of yourself you will be.

I couldn't believe that I actually accomplished this the first time I tried it. I truly told my brain "No!" When I went to bed the first night that I went a whole day without worrying, I felt as if I had conquered the world. My mind kept trying to get me to submit, but just like a spiritual fast from food, I just denied my flesh the chance by saying: "No! I am fasting anxiety. Help me, Jesus." The best part is, I probably called on the name of Jesus more times in that day than I ever had. I'm pretty sure it drove the devil crazy, and I love that. But I love even more how awesome our Jesus is. He never lets us down.

You have the power inside of you to win this battle. Scripture tells us, "But every spirit that does not acknowledge Jesus is not from God. This is the spirit of the antichrist, which you have heard is coming and even now is already in the world. You, dear children, are from God and have overcome them, because the one who is in you is greater than the one who is in the world" (1 John 4:3–4). My friend, memorize that! Meditate on those words and know in your heart of hearts that He who is in you is greater than that which is in the world. Get that down into your spirit.

You Have Authority

Know this: you do not have to keep succumbing to Satan's rule. Jesus already conquered Satan when He shed His blood for us. Let me tell you something, and I really want you to get this: there is power in the blood of Jesus to cast down strongholds. Say that out loud with me. *There is power in the blood of Jesus to cast down strongholds.* Say it again. *There is power in the blood of Jesus to cast down strongholds.* We do not have authority over Satan and his schemes because of anything we have done. But because of what Christ did for us, we have that power. Thank God for that every day.

My friend, learn how to tell Satan to get under your feet. Jesus did that, and He gave us that authority as a gift. We need to walk in that authority. When you feel an anxious thought or fear come over you, exercise your birthright and say to that stronghold, "Satan, get behind me in the name of Jesus." Immediately replace that thought with God's Word and quote whatever Scripture you have hidden in your heart at that time. I can usually quickly pull up some favorites, such as, "There is no fear in love. But perfect love drives out fear" (1 John 4:18) or "God hath not given us the spirit of fear, but of power, and of love, and of a sound mind" (2 Tim. 1:7, KJV).

We need to purposefully remind ourselves that God has given us a sound mind. Sometimes Satan will throw you into so much confusion that you will feel as if you have lost your mind. You have not lost your mind, my friend. You are just in a battle. You are in a battle, and you have the power to win it. You just need to drop the weapons you've been fighting with up until now that aren't working.

Some of these ineffectual weapons might be keeping quiet and not confessing sin to God or not sharing your struggles with a friend. (After all, you tell yourself, "You *know* she would never understand what you are going through!") It may be thoughts such as, "I am the only one who thinks like this" or "I just need to smile and pretend I am fine." Or your ineffectual weapon might sound like,

"I'll just take a couple pills to feel better" or "Oh, I just need some shopping therapy to get over this."

No, sweet friend, your weapon needs to be your sword, which is your Bible. Your weapon needs to be biblical knowledge, Scripture memorization, and learning to cast your cares on Jesus. Jesus already won the battle. You aren't called to fight alone. You need to stand behind Him and put on your armor.

Jesus—Your Armor Bearer

Jesus has His armor on, and He wants to be your armor bearer. In biblical days, when men went into battle, they always had an armor bearer who fought right in front of their leader, no matter where the battle would lead. The armor bearer carried the king's armor into battle so that by the time the king arrived at the battle, the king had energy to fight. The armor bearer stuck closer than a brother to the king.

If you can believe it—and I hope you will!—the Creator of the universe wants to be your armor bearer. His Word says in James 4:8, "Come near to God and he will come near to you." My pastor used to say that God wants us so close to Him that He can press His face up against our cheeks and snuggle us as we would our children.

Ephesians 6:10–18 reads:

> Finally, be strong in the Lord and in his mighty power. Put on the full armor of God, so that you can take your stand against the devil's schemes. For our struggle is not against flesh and blood, but against the rulers, against the authorities, against

> the powers of this dark world and against the spiritual forces of evil in the heavenly realms.
>
> Therefore put on the full armor of God, so that when the day of evil comes, you may be able to stand your ground, and after you have done everything, to stand. Stand firm then, with the belt of truth buckled around your waist, with the breastplate of righteousness in place, and with your feet fitted with the readiness that comes from the gospel of peace. In addition to all this, take up the shield of faith, with which you can extinguish all the flaming arrows of the evil one. Take the helmet of salvation and the sword of the Spirit, which is the Word of God.
>
> And pray in the Spirit on all occasions with all kinds of prayers and requests. With this in mind, be alert and always keep praying for all the Lord's people.

The truth is, these who are not "flesh and blood" are demons over which Satan has control. These demons are very real. We face a powerful army whose goal is the demolition of Christ's church. When we follow Christ, these demons become our enemies.

We must not fear this battle, though, because of what Jesus says to Peter in Matthew 16:18: "On this rock I will build my church, and the gates of Hades will not overcome it." Did you hear that? The gates of Hades will not overcome you! You are going to win this battle in your mind if you arm yourself correctly, stand firm in the faith, and grab hold of your armor bearer and never let Him go. However, my friend, you have to trust in the saving power of Jesus Christ.

Believe me, I know what this battle is like. Since I have been called into the ministry, Satan has not taken his ugly eyes off of me. He tries to get me to put those old shoes back on these new feet. He tries daily to get me to question my confidence in Christ, and he tries to get me to return to where I was before. But I refuse to submit to him, dear friend. I will not turn back! I have my eyes on Jesus, and Jesus hasn't taken His eyes off of me.

The Apostle Paul says in Acts 20:24, "However, I consider my life worth nothing to me; my only aim is to finish the race and complete the task the Lord Jesus has given me—the task of testifying to the good news of God's grace." Sometimes when the warfare seems overwhelming, I remind myself that there are still a lot of hurting people out there who need to hear the truth. If Satan can get me to question my birthright, then many lost souls will stay trapped in their sin. So I must stand firm—and so must you. Will you stand firm with me? Will you allow God to let Him build His church with you as one of the cornerstones? Don't let Satan steal that from you.

Flee the Flesh

Now let's take a lesson from the example of Paul and his young disciple Timothy. In the first letter he wrote to Timothy, Paul tells him, "Fight the good fight of the faith. Take hold of the eternal life to which you were called when you made your good confession in the presence of many witnesses" (1 Tim. 6:12). Oh, I love this passage! Prior to this verse, Paul had just talked to Timothy about not being swayed by the love of money. He was explaining contentment, not saying that money is evil, but rather the love of money. He was trying to keep Timothy protected from that.

In the verse before Paul talks about fighting the good fight, he says, "But you, man of God, flee from all of this, and pursue righteousness, godliness, faith, love, endurance and gentleness." He's like, "Watch how you start to feel about money, and pursue righteousness." Now this was quite obviously a decision that Timothy would have to make. He would have to flee from one and pursue another, and this would take a little bit of fighting. And this fighting is something we're familiar with, aren't we?

Now Paul was only talking about the love of money here, but we have so many other things that our flesh (our sin nature) desires that is contrary to what the Spirit desires, and we have to flee from the first and pursue the things of the second—the Spirit. Does this mean we have to literally run? Maybe from some things. It depends on what your flesh may be vying for that is contrary to the Spirit. If you have a drinking problem and you are walking by a bar and you feel your flesh tempting you to walk in, I'm going to tell you to run. Run as if you are being chased! If it's those cookies, and you are trying to do a gluten-free diet, I'm going to tell you to run away from that pantry and toward the blueberries.

Paul tells Timothy to take hold of the eternal life to which he was called when he made his good confession. What is that good confession? We all have to make this confession if we want to see Jesus face-to-face someday and walk into the gates of heaven when we die. That confession is that Jesus is Lord! That is the good confession Paul is talking about. Confessing and making Jesus Lord of our lives changes everything for us, starting with our salvation, our names being written in the Lamb's Book of Life, and then how we live while we are here.

Arm Yourself

But taking hold of the eternal life to which we were called involves some fighting. We will have to fight our flesh, and we will have to fight temptation from the enemy. We will have to fight living as the world does.

How do we arm ourselves? I know I might sound like a broken record chapter after chapter here, but I will never stop telling you that you arm yourself from the attack of the enemy by daily renewing your mind in the Word of God and by prayer. It's not just about reading the Word and praying, but praying and studying the Word every day.

You will also have to learn how to say the Word out loud at the enemy. The Word says, "Faith comes by hearing, and hearing by the Word of God" (Rom. 10:17, NKJV). We must say truths out loud to ourselves so that it comes out of our mouths, goes into our ears, and penetrates the heart. Our hearts are obstinate. They want what they want. Our emotions and intellect weren't changed at the moment of our good confession—only our Spirit was. The Word spoken out loud over our own lives, then, is what changes our souls and brings our bodies into submission.

Paul says, "So I say, walk by the Spirit, and you will not gratify the desires of the flesh. For the flesh desires what is contrary to the Spirit, and the Spirit what is contrary to the flesh. They are in conflict with each other" (Gal. 5:16–17). In other words, your own mind and body will fight against what God is trying to do in your Spirit. You have to crucify your old flesh and die to that old self every day so that you can live the life God desires you to live. It's not just about when you get to heaven, either. God wants you to be successful and victorious as a living Christian here on the earth.

I especially love how Paul says at the very end of that passage in Ephesians 6, "Oh, and pray all the time, everywhere." Do you think you can get away without praying, my friend? I wouldn't suggest it. I can't! I pray all day about everything—little prayers, big prayers, driving in the car prayers, in my kitchen cooking prayers, walking on the road prayers, in my Bible study chair prayers, and on my face with my dog looking at me as if I am dead prayers. Prayer is huge. I think that is why Paul lists it last—so we will remember it. He starts out with "Be strong in the Lord," and he ends with "Pray all the time." Why? Because in order to win, we have a secret weapon, and His name is Jesus! He is our ringer. He is our MVP and our go-to player. Apart from God, we can do nothing. But we learn from Philippians what we can accomplish with God: "I can do all this through him who gives me strength" (Phil. 4:13).

We fight the enemy with the Word and with the Lord. With that combination, we win! We fight the enemy's attempts to get us dwelling on the mistakes of our past and our fears of the future by living daily—minute by minute, second by second—from faith to faith to faith in the strength of today. We fight the enemy by praying and talking to God each day, arming ourselves with the armor of God, reading, meditating on, and memorizing God's Word each day, and saying God's truths out loud so that He hears them and so they begin to penetrate our stubborn hearts.

Don't forget our secret weapon is Jesus. Fix your eyes on Jesus, and I promise you, you will be OK. Don't take your eyes off Him for a minute. He holds the keys to your peace and your victory. He already fought death and Hades, and now every knee must bow to Him. Why would we think we need more than Jesus?

Prison Ministry

Yesterday I sat in one of the most Spirit-filled, anointed church services I have ever attended in the chapel at the Coleman federal prison. It was actually the first time I had ever toured a prison, much less ministered there. And today I feel like I am forever changed. I woke up this morning with the beautiful faces of those women carved in my memory, and I couldn't help but thank God over and over that He encouraged me to go.

You see, with the anxiety that I have faced my entire life, even movies with prison scenes in them have caused me such pain to watch that I chose to never even consider visiting the lonely in prison. I must confess that whenever I read the scripture in Matthew 25:36 that said, "I needed clothes and you clothed me, I was sick and you looked after me, I was in prison and you came to visit me," I would silently say to God, "You know I love You. I promise I will take care of the sick and the hungry and give people water and food. But God, please don't make me go to the prisons." I am honest when I tell you I asked Him this over and over.

Then last night, on our way back from the prison, I said to Tommy, "He never made me go, hon. He loved me enough to make me *want* to go." That's the honest-to-God truth, my friends. I'm crying right now, thinking

God loves me so much that He wasn't just thinking about those women I was able to preach to, pray for, hug, cry with, and worship with. He was concerned that I overcome one of my worst fears and trust Him!

So today I am home celebrating a God who loves us too much not to run to us when we are still way off, then embracing us and growing us into the vessels that He created us to be. I am celebrating a God that allowed me the chance to pray with a woman to accept Jesus Christ as Lord and decide to follow Him for the rest of her life. Today I am celebrating a God who had me see these beautiful women as sisters in Christ, sisters who are just as forgiven by a perfect God as we are today, sisters who are in love with the same God that I am in love with, but maybe even a little freer than many of us because they spend so much time in the Word and in prayer each day! Today I am celebrating the power of the Word of God to heal the brokenhearted, break satanic strongholds, set the captives free, and give all of us a fresh start each day.

Thank You, God, for not pushing me to go. Thank You for loving me until I was ready to go! I love You, Jesus.

http://momydlo.wordpress.com
/2013/11/18/prison-ministry

Homework

Spend time in prayer as you answer the following questions.

1. *How comfortable are you with rebuking Satan and his demons?*

2. *When have you felt God fighting for you, as your armor bearer?*

3. *What spiritual battle are you experiencing in your life?*

4. *How have you been tempted to give up and give in to the devil and his schemes?*

5. *How determined are you to stand firm in the faith?*

Read the following scriptures and rewrite them in your own words:

- 1 John 4:3–4
- Mark 16:17
- 2 Corinthians 10:3–6
- Ephesians 6:10–18
- 1 John 4:18

Memorize

> There is no fear in love, but perfect love drives out fear, because fear has to do with punishment. The one who fears is not made perfect in love.
>
> —1 John 4:18

Confession

Practice saying out loud over and over this week: "I will not fear."

Application

Make a decision to fast from worry. Start with one day, and add days as you are successful.

Journal Time

This week, continue to write in your thankfulness journal. Talk to God about the spiritual warfare you have been experiencing.

Chapter 5

THE DEVIL IS A LIAR

ONE DAY I came home from work, and I was in "mom mode," getting the kids started on homework and chores. Then I felt some fears and anxieties come over me like a blanket. I began worrying about the kids. Things that might sound like: What if Eli doesn't start reading? He seems to be a little behind his friends. What if he has a learning disability? Maybe it was something I did when I was pregnant? Maybe I didn't eat as well as I did with the others? I love him so much. What if he doesn't get it? I probably don't spend as much reading time with him as I should. I'm sure I read more with the older kids. This is all my fault. What if? What if? What if?

I felt an instinct to panic and knew I'd better drop whatever I was doing and get in the Word. I told Eli to get his bike and head out back, and I would watch him ride his bike as I sat on the deck to read my Bible.

As I sat there watching him, I began to study. I had been reading Isaiah in my quiet time, and I kept hearing a still, small voice saying, "Strengthen your feeble arms and weak knees." Over and over those words kept coming into my spirit. I didn't know what that meant, and I thought I must have read it somewhere, so I put a bookmark in

Isaiah and looked those words up in the concordance in the back of my Bible.

As I looked under the word *strengthen*, the last scripture on the list said "strengthen your feeble arms and weak knees," so I immediately turned to the passage it referenced in Hebrews 12:12. I read the whole scripture out loud, which says, "Strengthen your feeble arms and weak knees. 'Make level paths for your feet,' so that the lame may not be disabled, but rather healed" (vv. 12–13).

I looked up to the sky and said, "God, You need me to get stronger so other people can get healed, right?"

I read the commentary at the bottom of my Bible and it said, "God is not only a disciplining parent, but also a demanding coach who pushes us to our limits and requires our lives to be disciplined. Although we do not feel strong enough to push on to victory, we will be able to accomplish it as we follow Christ and draw on His strength. Then we can use our growing strength to help those around us who are weak and struggling."[1]

My dear friend, I believe what Isaiah 50:4 says. It says, "The Sovereign LORD has given me a well-instructed tongue, to know the word that sustains the weary." What it means is that God is trying to heal *you*, and unless *I* work hard and do what *I* know to be right, *you* can't experience the healing God has for *you*. So I am making a promise to you right now, and I am not giving up. I believe there is victory for every believer who simply won't give up.

I am never going to give up on God's Word. I am never going to give up on His promises to me. I am never going to give up on the destiny that I have as a child of God. I want you to say out loud right now to yourself too: "I am not going to give up!" Say it out loud again, child of

God: "I am not going to give up!" Awesome job! Thank You, Jesus!

But the story gets even better, and I want you to see how cool God is. After I realized God's revelation for me was just what I needed to hear to get right back to studying and writing, I looked at the top of the page in my Bible where I had turned, and I had written at one time, "Isaiah 61:7–8." God then took me right back to where I had been studying in Isaiah!

If I weren't able to distinguish God's voice in my life, I would have missed that fresh revelation from Him! He speaks to us through His Word. Isaiah 61:7 reads, "Instead of your shame you will receive a double portion, and instead of disgrace you will rejoice in your inheritance. And so you will inherit a double portion in your land, and everlasting joy will be yours." Do you want everlasting joy to be yours? Everlasting joy is joy that doesn't depend on circumstances. It is joy that, no matter what our feelings tell us, we can stay in peace. That is a promise from God. Let's receive that from Him. Don't turn down your gifts from your daddy. He wants to bless you, but you can't give up.

His Native Language

Do you realize you believe lies? If you are reading this book, I already know that you believe lies, because anxiety is a lie in itself about how much control we actually have over our lives. But read what Matthew 6:25–34 tells us about that:

> Therefore I tell you, do not worry about your life, what you will eat or drink; or about your body, what you will wear. Is not life more than food, and the

> body more than clothes? Look at the birds of the air; they do not sow or reap or store away in barns, and yet your heavenly Father feeds them. Are you not much more valuable than they? Can any one of you by worrying add a single hour to your life?
>
> And why do you worry about clothes? See how the flowers of the field grow. They do not labor or spin. Yet I tell you that not even Solomon in all his splendor was dressed like one of these. If that is how God clothes the grass of the field, which is here today and tomorrow is thrown into the fire, will he not much more clothe you—you of little faith? So do not worry, saying, "What shall we eat?" or "What shall we drink?" or "What shall we wear?" For the pagans run after all of these things, and your heavenly Father knows that you need them. But seek first His kingdom and His righteousness, and all these things will be given to you as well. Therefore do not worry about tomorrow, for tomorrow will worry about itself. Each day has enough trouble of its own.

How much control do we actually have over our lives, dear friend? I mean, if God decides to feed us, are we going to eat? And if God decides to clothe us, are we going to be clothed? (Unless you are in the bathtub reading this, I am assuming you are clothed right now!)

We are being lied to on a daily basis. And because we struggle with anxiety, we believe the lie that we control our lives. Satan whispers lies like this to us in our spirits, and we have heard and believed those lies for so long that we don't even recognize they're lies anymore. God's Word says in John 8:44, "He was a murderer from the beginning, not holding to the truth, for there is no truth in him.

When he lies, he speaks his native language, for he is a liar and the father of lies."

Satan has a plan for your life. His plan is to steal, kill, and destroy (John 10:10). That is all he knows. When he lies and kills, he speaks his native language. I know that is not very comforting, but you need to be on your guard against the enemy's lies. You can have victory over Satan's lies because you are saved. You are not just saved to escape hell. You are also saved to be set free. Jesus says, "If you hold to my teaching, you are really my disciples. Then you will know the truth, and the truth will set you free" (John 8:31–32). So here is the key, my friend. Hold to Jesus's teaching, and you will begin to recognize truths and put to death the lies of the enemy.

When Feelings Lie

Now, let's talk about our feelings lying to us for one second. Your feelings cannot be trusted. Feelings change like a teenager changes cell phones. We cannot act on feelings. Our feelings are affected by our appetites, our hormones, our energy levels...you name it. I know the Sovereign Lord has given me an instructed tongue (Isa. 50:4), but do I feel this all of the time? No! Actually 90 percent of the time I feel the opposite. I feel inadequate, insecure, and unworthy. Maybe you do too. But I have learned not to believe in my feelings because they lie to me. You cannot wait for your feelings to line up with the Word of God. You just have to line up your actions and decisions with the Word of God first.

You see, the enemy feeds countless lies to our feelings—feelings that might sound like:

- You are the only one who thinks like this.
- You will never overcome these feelings. You might as well give in to them.
- You are no good. No one loves you.
- You are alone. No one will see.
- You must not even be saved, or you wouldn't think like this.
- You're never going to get healed. Quit looking like a fool, thinking God is going to heal you. God's too busy for your little problems.
- You're the worst wife and the worst mother.
- You're going to mess this thing up for good.

Lie after lie after lie. My friend, the worst part is, we start to believe him. Satan's warfare begins in our thinking. And one of Satan's easiest tricks is to convince us to follow our feelings.

Are you constantly reacting and submitting to your feelings? If so, please take this piece of advice that will serve you well, even if you ignore the rest of what I teach in this entire book: *Don't trust your feelings!* Our feelings are affected by everything, from our hormones to what we have or have not eaten that day, from the weather to the devil himself. How I would love to tell you that once you make Jesus Lord of your life and you decide to follow Him, every part of you begins to submit to His leadership. But that would be a lie. The truth is that our feelings have a mind of their own because they are born of our flesh and have only ever answered to our flesh, which gets its cues from our five senses.

The Word is specific about the struggle we face in our flesh, trying to get our feelings to play nice. In Romans 7:21–24 the Apostle Paul explains this struggle: "So I find this law at work: Although I want to do good, evil is there with me. For in my inner being I delight in God's law; but I see another law at work in me, waging war against the law of my mind and making me a prisoner of the law of sin at work within me. What a wretched man I am!" To counter this reality, you need to be daily telling yourself truths that your feelings need to be reminded of each day—truths such as *God loves me, God loves me, God loves me, and God's not mad at me.*

My friend, God is not mad at you. He's mad *about* you! You see, this is just one example of the way our feelings lie to us and how the enemy of our souls uses those feelings against us. He tries to get us to believe God is mad at us, when the truth is that God is crazy about us! My friend, you must get clear on the way your feelings can warp the truth. You must learn from their lies and begin to live in the truth.

Counter His Lies With the Truth

Here's the real deal about all this. If you are consistently in the Word of God, you will begin to recognize the difference between truths and lies. But until you digest enough of God's Word, you will struggle with even knowing you are being lied to.

God's Word is 100 percent truth. If we think about something and wonder if it is truth or simply a lie or trap from the enemy, we must search for our answers in God's

Word. If our thoughts contradict what God's Word tells us, we need to recognize that we are being lied to, and we have to take control of our thinking. Second Corinthians 10:5 reads, "We demolish arguments and every pretension that sets itself up against the knowledge of God, and we take captive every thought to make it obedient to Christ." We need to know what God's knowledge is, and we learn that by studying His Word. By studying daily His truths, we will recognize the things that set themselves up against those truths. We will know those thoughts are lies.

So let's do a little exercise. From this exercise you will be able to see how knowing the truth allows us to see where Satan contradicts those truths with lies to get us off God's path for our lives. We'll look at a lie and then counter it with the truth of Scripture.

Lie #1: You'll never amount to much. You're just a housewife.

Truth: God's Word says in Proverbs 31:27–30, "She watches over the affairs of her household and does not eat the bread of idleness. Her children arise and call her blessed; her husband also, and he praises her: 'Many women do noble things, but you surpass them all.' Charm is deceptive, and beauty is fleeting; but a woman who fears the LORD is to be praised."

I have been a wife and mother for over twenty-two years now. Throughout this time I have worked in and out of corporate America. I have started and directed several not-for-profit organizations. I have owned my own business, worked at home and away from home. I have worked with the elderly, with children, and with people my own age. My friend, I can honestly tell you that the most inspiring, the most difficult, and the most important job I have ever had is to love and honor my husband and care for my four precious gifts from God. I'm eternally grateful that they are all walking with the Lord and seeking Him for their futures. Raising godly children in a negative world and loving, supporting, and encouraging your husband is not a part-time job or a hobby. You are not "just a housewife"! It is the most precious ministry you could ever have.

Lie #2: You're going to mess up your life. You're going to make one bad decision and ruin everything.

Truth: God's Word says, "He will not let your foot slip—he who watches over you will not slumber.... The Lord will watch over your coming and going both now and forevermore" (Ps. 121:3, 8). You aren't going to mess up. You have self-control. It's a fruit of the Spirit. But if we slip even a little, He picks us up.

Lie #3: God can't forgive you for what you've done. And God doesn't heal anymore.

Truth: God's Word says, in Psalm 103:2–4, "Praise the Lord, my soul, and forget not all his benefits—who forgives all your sins and heals all your diseases, who redeems your life from the pit." You are worthy of forgiveness. There's nothing you could have done that could negate God's ability to forgive. No sin is stronger than the blood of Jesus.

Lie #4: Your lost child is gone. He'll never return to the faith.

Truth: God's Word says, "Train up a child in the way he should go, and when he is old he will not depart from it"

(Prov. 22:6, NKJV). Keep praying! Keep believing! It doesn't say when they are young they won't turn; it says, when they are old. Give them time, prayers, and love, and God will do the rest.

Lie #5: God has forgotten about you. He doesn't care about your future.

Truth: God's Word says, "'For I know the plans I have for you,' declares the LORD, 'plans to prosper you and not to harm you, plans to give you hope and a future'" (Jer. 29:11). My friend, the best is yet to come...your future. You have one in Him. Trust Jesus with your future. He is such an awesome planner.

All these are but a glimpse of the lies that most of us have believed at one time or another. But do you see how Satan tries to tell you the exact opposite of what God has in store for you? It is because he speaks his native language when he lies. Billy Graham describes the devil in *Peace With God* this way: "He is a prince of lofty stature, of unlimited craft and cunning, able to take advantage of every opportunity that presents itself, able to turn every situation to his own advantage. He is unrelenting and cruel."[2]

Three Steps to Fight Satan

The three steps you can take to fight bondage of any kind and stay in the light are (1) rebuke Satan in the name of Jesus, (2) call on the Word, and (3) stand your ground. Let's look at each one in turn.

Step 1: Rebuke Satan in the name of Jesus

If what you hear does not agree with everything you have learned in God's Word, it most likely is a lie. Once you recognize the thought you are thinking is a lie or a trap, you need to cast Satan away from you by calling on the name of Jesus. We have more power in His name than all of Satan's demons combined. Tell him to get behind you, in Jesus's name, and rebuke him and the lie.

James 4:7 says, "Submit yourselves, then, to God. Resist the devil, and he will flee from you." Oh my goodness, he has to flee! Use your birthright and cast him away and call on the name of Jesus. Please grasp in your spirit the strength you have in that name. The Word says that one day every knee will bow and every tongue will confess that Jesus is Lord (Phil. 2:9–11). You need to confess it now. When you do, you will never be the same. It is one of God's commandments to not use the Lord's name in vain (Exod. 20:7). I know God is concerned not only with His name not being used as a curse word, but also with the strength He knows gains force in the heavenly realms when Jesus's name is used in battle. That is why even using His name flippantly, with a phrase such as OMG, is an abomination to Him. We are blessed and honored to be able to call on His name for healing, protection, salvation, and strength. Realize the power in His name and use it to defeat the devil and his demons.

Step 2: Call on the Word

After you have exercised your true authority, you then have to pull out your sword—the Word of God—to fight. Call up any scripture you can think of. Hide some scriptures in your pocket or purse. Pin them up wherever you are until they well up out of you naturally to fight.

I'm right here with you in this work. For example, as I was writing this chapter, Satan was trying to come at me with some old junk that I used to believe. I began to hear the enemy saying: "They don't care about anything you have to say. You don't have a degree in counseling. You're just a wimpy worrier who still deals with this stuff if you don't study enough. You should be well by now. What a fake." I had to immediately say, "I am not putting those old shoes on these new feet." Then I had to get into the Word so deep and draw on the most powerful strength I have: His Word. I was on my way to work soon, and I knew I'd better stay plugged into Him. I found a scripture that was speaking to me, and I opened it up. I read it at stoplights, meditated on it the whole drive, and when I got into work, that Word spoke to me all day. I was able to do my work and not be distracted by Satan's evil schemes.

We fight the enemy and win when we fight the way Jesus fought. Let's take a look at what He did:

> Then Jesus was led by the Spirit into the wilderness to be tempted by the devil. After fasting forty days and forty nights, he was hungry. The tempter came to him and said, "If you are the Son of God, tell these stones to become bread."
>
> Jesus answered, "It is written: 'Man shall not live on bread alone, but on every word that comes from the mouth of God.'"
>
> Then the devil took him to the holy city and had him stand on the highest point of the temple. "If you are the Son of God," he said, "throw yourself down. For it is written:
>
> 'He will command his angels concerning you, and they will lift you up in their hands, so that you will not strike your foot against a stone.'"
>
> Jesus answered him, "It is also written: 'Do not put the Lord your God to the test.'"

> Again, the devil took him to a very high mountain and showed him all the kingdoms of the world and their splendor. "All this I will give you," he said, "if you will bow down and worship me."
>
> Jesus said to him, "Away from me, Satan! For it is written: 'Worship the Lord your God, and serve him only.'"
>
> Then the devil left him, and angels came and attended him.
>
> —MATTHEW 4:1–11

We learn how to fight the enemy correctly by following the perfect example of Jesus. Jesus rebuked Satan. In verse 10 He says, "Away from me, Satan!" Because of Jesus's authority, He had the power to tell Satan where to go and what to do. We have that same power when we rebuke the enemy in Jesus's name. It is not in our own power. It is in the power of the name of Jesus. Jesus called on the Word. Jesus quoted Scripture at the devil. Three very powerful words that we need to learn are *it is written*.

As you can see, the devil is such a liar and counterfeiter that in verse 6, he tries to confuse even Jesus with Scripture. Dear friend, be on your guard. The enemy knows the Word. He will even try to confuse us sometimes with the Word. That is why we need to be armed with the power of the name of Jesus as well. Satan is powerless when confronted with the name of Jesus and the Word used together.

Step 3: Stand your ground

Our final step is to stand firm. We can learn how to fight the enemy by fighting as Jesus did. Jesus knew how to stand firm. Notice that the devil didn't leave at Jesus's first rebuke of him with Scripture. It took three different scriptures until the enemy realized Jesus meant business before he left Him and the angels showed up to attend Jesus.

Quite honestly it is the standing firm step that is usually the hardest. Standing firm is all about trust. The devil wants us to question that trust at every turn. We have to plant our feet in the truth and decide not to waver. Rebuking the enemy and calling on the Word can be done by anyone, regardless of the size of their faith. They are intellectual steps. Standing our ground requires strong faith, and that's a spiritual step. It is our outward sign to the enemy that we trust in the name of Jesus and the Word of God. Our ability to stand firm is strengthened every time we battle the devil's lies the way Jesus did.

Fighting as Jesus fought brings us into the peace that passes all understanding with God and under His wing where we find refuge. You will experience the truth in God's Word that says, "Where the spirit of the Lord is, there is liberty" (2 Cor. 3:17).

When the Enemy Is You

You know, sometimes we aren't even fighting the enemy. Sometimes we are our own worst enemy. I know I am mine. A lot of my struggles come from poor thinking patterns, such as trying to reason everything to death. When I try to reason things out, absent of the Lord's help, I am too inclined to fall into anxiety. While I am relentlessly obsessing on a matter, whatever it is, I become sure that if I can recall enough details of something I should be able to calm myself down from walking into an anxiety attack—when in all actuality my obsessive reasoning causes me to focus more on lies and perpetual problems than on truth. My reasoning fixes my eyes on the problem instead of fixing my eyes on Jesus, who could blot my problem out in the blink of an eye. Isaiah 1:18 actually tells us, "'Come now, and let us reason together,' says the LORD" (NKJV). The Lord wants to help us reason out the matter at hand without getting hung up on details we may misperceive.

The Apostle Paul says in 1 Corinthians 13:11, "When I was a child, I talked like a child, I thought like a child, I reasoned like a child. When I became a man, I put the ways of childhood behind me." As we mature as Christians, we are to mature in how we process thoughts. Children are usually void of a filter on their mouths. They say what they think, and they think about whatever pops into their minds. What if we decided that to grow up spiritually means that we take some responsibility for what we think about? What if we put childish, unfiltered ways behind us and chose instead to reason with the Lord and not ourselves? What if when our thinker decides to take a reasoning detour, we put up a spiritual stop sign and say, "No, I choose to reason with the Lord"? I have decided to think about whatever is true and real. We will see in a later chapter that the only truth we are able to recognize is whatever is sitting right in front of us in the present.

In the natural I have a terrible habit of trying to figure out the answers to every question. I get hung up on the details of why, who, and how long. This is what I like to call my "overactive figure-outer." If we do not deliberately choose to reason with the Lord instead, we will be left to our own underactive or overactive "figure-outers," leading us back down the agonizing trail toward anxiety.

We must talk as mature adults, think as mature adults, and reason as mature adults. Let's join Paul and put childish ways behind us, choosing to reason with the Lord instead. We must be OK telling ourselves over and over, "No! I choose to reason with the Lord."

Reasoning with the Lord does not mean we throw a prayer up in the air for two seconds and then obsess about our problem or fear for two hours, then pray another prayer again. Reasoning with the Lord must be deliberate. You will need self-control to say no to the imaginations and yes to saturating yourself in the Word.

You can beat Satan at his own game by knowing truth and hiding it in your heart. Psalm 119:11 says, "I have hidden your word in my heart that I might not sin against you." God's Word is meant to be imprinted on our very being. We need to be a wellspring of truth. There needs to be so much truth hiding in our hearts that there is no room for lies.

Again, this will take time. We want a get-well-quick scheme, but God wants a changed heart. If you are forty years old, sweet friend, you have forty years of lies that you need to replace with truths. That doesn't happen overnight, but you can enjoy the journey on your way to freedom. Galatians 6:9 reads, "Let us not become weary in doing good, for at the proper time we will reap a harvest if we do not give up." You just have to hang in there. Begin to recognize where things you believe about yourself don't line up with God's truths—they are lies. Once you recognize you are being lied to, you are on the right path toward healing.

Make a pact with yourself that you are not going to give up the fight. You have to fight with your sword in hand. Arm yourself with the Word. Learn the Word. Recognize the lies. Stop letting Satan win. Stop playing around with the enemy!

Rebuke Satan with the name of Jesus, call on the Word, and stand your ground. Make a pact that you will put childish ways behind you, and begin to think as an adult.

Your thoughts do not have to control you. You are in complete control of them. Say no to reasoning on your own.

Perfect Love Casts Out Fear

I recently gave a message on overcoming fear, and guess what I struggled with two nights later? Fear. Gripping, irrational fears in the middle of the night that were trying to steal my sleep and peace. So, I put on my armor, and I started to fight. I began rebuking the enemy and throwing verses at the devil in Jesus's name. I kept quoting Psalm 91 out loud. But time just kept crawling and the clock just kept flashing as the hours passed and I was still up.

Then I heard God say to me, "How much do you love Delaney?" (That is my sweet niece who was having a sleepover at our house.) He said, "How much did you love taking her and Eli to the park today and laughing? And how much do you love Eli?"

I just kept hearing God show me in tangible ways people that I love. He said, "Think about that love."

I started thinking about the love I have for my husband and my kids and my nephews and nieces and how I would lay down my life for them. I started thinking about times I have cuddled them and pushed them on swings and played with finger paints and Play-Doh with them. Then, before I knew it, it was morning.

I told Tommy the next morning over coffee, "God just kept telling me, 'Think about this, think about that.'" I told him how cool it was. But I have to be honest. I am a little thick sometimes. It wasn't until later that I realized this was the "perfect love" God is talking about in the Bible! It's a pure, unconditional, willing to lay down your life for those you love kind of love. That is God's love! That is perfect love. And that kind of love sends those fear demons running.

http://momydlo.wordpress.com/2013/10/28/perfect-love-casts-out-fear/

Homework

Spend time in prayer as you answer the following questions.

1. *What feelings/activities seem to trigger your anxiety? (This may show you where you tend to believe lies.)*

2. *When Satan is keeping you up at night, what are the words he whispers to you? (This may show you what lies you tend to believe.)*

3. *What steps will you take to fight the enemy and win?*

4. *What scripture can you use to combat his tactics?*

5. *Where are you still attempting to reason your problems alone without consulting the Lord?*

Read the following scriptures and rewrite them in your own words:

- Isaiah 61:7–8

- Matthew 6:25–34

- John 8:31–32

- 2 Corinthians 10:5

- Hosea 11:4

- James 4:7

Memorize

Submit yourselves, then, to God. Resist the devil, and he will flee from you.

—James 4:7

Confession

Practice saying out loud over and over this week: "Satan is a liar! God's Word is truth. I believe the truth!"

Application

Create your scripture cards and put them everywhere you need them.

Journal Time

This week continue to write ten things you are thankful for in your thankfulness journal, and tell God what lies you have been believing.

Chapter 6

BREAKING SATANIC STRONGHOLDS

As you crack open this chapter, keep in mind that the message contained in it is detrimental to the enemy and the gates of hell. I know with everything I am that the devil does not want you to know that you can be set free from strongholds of the mind. I took one for the team in writing this chapter. Want proof? The month I wrote this chapter, here's what happened:

- I counted five godly confrontations and uncomfortable conversations I had to have with other believers, all of which (thankfully!) ended in love.
- The outright flu demon attacked my family. Each one of us came down with it.
- My husband and I had an embarrassing moment at a party. (I can't even give details it was so embarrassing.)
- I had to apologize to my daughter's coach for being a little overzealous at her basketball game. The coach didn't even know I was being judgmental and telling other parents how she should coach, but God made me

confess and apologize to her the next day anyway.

- My nine-year-old son, Eli, got hurt playing two-hand touch football and cut his head open on Super Bowl Sunday, so we spent the night in the emergency room getting staples in his head.
- Even after we all fought the flu, a stomach virus came through the Mydlo home, and half my family caught that. My OCD kicked into full force with bleach and Lysol.

Just when I was excited about leaving the house after we weren't contagious anymore, I backed out of my driveway and hit my brother-in-law's car, which was in my blind spot. My friend, the enemy is a piler. Oh, he loves to work his annoying torment on top of an already frustrated, tired, and weary believer. He is no gentleman, and he will attempt to strike when you are at your weakest. Hopefully this list I've shared with you is proof that I know this from experience!

But in that particular month I just kept fighting our enemy with the weapons God showed me to fight with: prayer, the Word of God, and truth affirmations. I'm going to teach you how to fight him this same way. Are you ready to fight? I hope so. Because we are warriors in God's army, and we are equipped to win. We just have to put on our armor and know how to battle God's way!

Defining Strongholds

First of all, you might not know what a stronghold is, much less if Satan has created a stronghold in your life, so let's start there.

When I did some research on the word *stronghold*, I was blown away by what the word's definition revealed about the pride and deception of the enemy. In my concordance, for example, the word *stronghold* has two definitions: (1) a place or means of protection or refuge and (2) Satan's power. Do you see how those are two completely different things?

Let's take a closer look. In Psalm 144 David refers to the Lord, saying, "He is my loving God and my fortress, my stronghold and my deliverer, my shield, in whom I take refuge" (v. 2). Obviously David is using the word *stronghold* here to describe the protection God provides for him. In 2 Samuel 22:3 David this time sings the words of this song as he has seen the Lord deliver him from danger: "The LORD is my rock, my fortress and my deliverer; my God is my rock, in whom I take refuge, my shield and the horn of my salvation. He is my stronghold, my refuge and my savior."

Dear friend, there is no doubt that God is the stronghold we are to run to in times of trouble, loneliness, affliction, trials...you name it. He is our place of protection. The question is: Why is the second definition of *stronghold* "Satan's power"? I am going to go out on a spiritual limb here with God and tell you, based on everything I know about how the enemy works in the lives of believers and unbelievers, it is because he is a counterfeiter and a liar. The enemy tries to counterfeit everything God intends for our good, and he does it so as to destroy us. The enemy lures you away from your safe place—your stronghold, which is the Lord—with lies, manipulation, and deception, and then he begins to have power.

So the enemy's first tactic is to pull you away from the Lord, your stronghold. Since born-again believers filled with the Spirit are never actually separate from the Spirit because God promises He will never leave us nor forsake us (Deut. 31:6), the devil has to lie to you to get you to believe you are on your own. He has to manipulate you into a mental cave and get you to believe you are in this fight alone. And if we fall into the trap of believing that lie, he gains power.

Some of his strength, though, comes from his patience. He waits until we are weak, tired, and weary, and then he pounces. The Word says he is like a roaring lion, seeking whom he may devour (1 Pet. 5:8). If you know anything about lions, you know they don't usually attack their prey when they are among herds or traveling with the strength of a pack. They wait for the lonely, isolated animal all by itself that has wandered away from the pack, and then they pounce. That is why Satan waits for you to take your eyes off Jesus for a second, to forget who your stronghold is, to skip a few days in the Word, and then he begins to lie and lie and lie. When we are caught with our armor off, he shoots his fiery darts, and we find ourselves bloody and limping.

How Strongholds Gain Entry

Strongholds begin when we give Satan permission to enter our lives through disobedience or offense. Now this disobedience can be something we view as harmless as worrying. But the truth is that God's Word tells us over and over to cast our cares upon God (1 Pet. 5:7) and not to be anxious about anything, but in everything to pray and lift our requests up to God (Phil. 4:6–7). When we worry anyway, we are in disobedience.

We have to remind ourselves that controlling behaviors such as worry and anxiety are something God warns us about in His Word, and we have to do everything in our power to fight them, because when we start worrying, we give the enemy power to work.

Other acts of disobedience or offense may be unforgiveness toward others or ourselves. When we don't allow ourselves to forgive those who have hurt us or forgive ourselves for the sins God has already forgiven when we have truly repented, we leave the door open for the enemy to work. He comes in and feeds on guilt—the guilt of those who hurt us or our own guilt we won't let go of—and he gains strength.

Personally that's the fight I fight on a regular basis in my spirit. I feel guilty all of the time. When the wind blows, I feel guilty. When anything bad happens in the world, the enemy lies and tells me I could somehow have stopped it and didn't. I am constantly fighting the bondage of guilt with the Word of truth, affirmations, and prayer.

Speaking of guilt, I had a supernatural thing happen to me that helped me better understand it, and I am so grateful God showed it to me. I was cleaning my house, making my son's bed, and said to myself, "Oh, yeah, God told me to research *imagined guilt*." I kept cleaning a little and then thought to myself, "I don't even know when God told me that. Was it in my sleep or in my study?" I couldn't put my thoughts around it, so I knew it was supernatural.

I finished cleaning, sat down, and googled *imagined guilt.* Do you know what I discovered? That it's a true disorder the secular world has come up with to explain why we feel guilty when we haven't done anything wrong.

As Christians we understand that in the natural world when someone tells someone something enough times, they start to believe it about themselves. It is called a self-fulfilling prophecy. This is happening in the supernatural world as well. The enemy lies to us so many times, saying, "You are guilty, you are guilty, you are guilty," that we begin to believe we are guilty! It is basically believing lies until they become the truth to us. Satan is the accuser of the brethren, and we are the brethren he is accusing. If we hear the lies enough and we believe them enough, he creates a stronghold.

Sometimes strongholds are created because of sins we don't want to stop doing. We really like gossiping with girlfriends at the hairdresser's or the coffee bar, or we like flirting with the guy at work. "After all," we rationalize, "it's harmless, and we are both married and would never overstep that boundary." Or we question, "What's the big deal with not submitting to my husband? I'm really more of a leader anyway, and he needs me to boss him around. He isn't the leader type."

If you have ever heard the phrase "Don't give the devil an inch or he will become your ruler," that is exactly what happens when we give the enemy access to our lives through offense and disobedience. Ephesians 4:26–27 says, "'In your anger, do not sin': Do not let the sun go down while you are still angry, and do not give the devil a foothold." In thinking about the pits that I have landed in, courtesy of the enemy, a foothold is a perfect analogy. I can just picture myself trying to run from him, but he has ahold of my leg and won't let me go. He holds on to us as if our feet are stuck in quicksand.

Now what do I mean by *offense*? The word *offense* means a violation or an act that leads to disapproval. Ladies, we can be physically offended by someone, emotionally offended by someone, or sexually offended by someone. We can even be spiritually offended by someone, and I am going to tell you that can be one of the toughest offenses to overcome. The enemy has a wonderful time with that one because he loves disunity among believers. If he can divide us, he can try to conquer. That is why I feel so strongly about Christians supporting and attending interdenominational studies and events whenever they can. This allows God's family to worship together despite preferences and doctrinal differences. Then it's all about our daddy and not us.

Let me tell you something. If you do not have a stronghold already constructed because of the offense of someone else or yourself, the devil will try to offend you with temptation to get you to a place of submission so he can create a stronghold in your life. But remember that he has no power unless we give it to him.

How Strongholds Work

Since the enemy is a counterfeiter, he uses strongholds in us to set himself up as an opponent to God. In 2 Corinthians 10:5 it says that a stronghold includes "arguments and every pretension that sets itself up against the knowledge of God." What the devil is trying to do is steal our mental, physical, emotional, and spiritual energy so that the abundant life God has intended for us is strangled.

That is his motive. He knows that when you have given your life to Jesus and begun your new life in Christ, he only has this life to torment you. He knows you have an eternity of joy and peace and happiness in your new home in heaven, and he wants to steal whatever confidence you have in the calling God has for you. He does this to distract you from sharing Christ with others by getting you to feel fear, insecurity, or pure exhaustion.

Dear friend, here is some good news: we are not controlled by the enemy. Let me say that again: *we are not under the control of the enemy!* We have to learn how to shut the door on him once and for all so we can walk in the freedom Christ has for us, live out the calling God has for us, and enjoy our lives while we are here. Yes, it is OK to enjoy your life. Jesus said, "I came so that you may have life, and have it in abundance" (John 10:10). That's the good news. The Lord is our stronghold, and we don't have to be bound in satanic strongholds any longer.

How to Break Strongholds

People of faith, it is our responsibility to break the strongholds of the enemy so we can live in the freedom Christ has for us. It is God's will for us to live in freedom. The Word says in Galatians 5, "It is for freedom that Christ has set us free.... Do not let yourselves be burdened again by a yoke of slavery" (v. 1).

But we cannot just pray strongholds off of us. Strongholds will not bow down to prayer alone. Prayer, in and of itself, will not break a stronghold, but prayer is *part* of breaking a stronghold. We also can't just become biblical scholars, believing that if we have enough of God's Word in our brains we will be free. Biblical knowledge alone is not enough, either. Puffed-up biblical scholars who are full of head knowledge but have no heart are usually so bound by the enemy that it would floor you. But learning to meditate upon, memorize, and confess God's Word is a huge *part* of breaking strongholds off us too. And lastly, we could say positive affirmations out loud all day long and it would not kill our strongholds, either. Those positive affirmations would become mere useless chatter if we didn't add them to the other two steps needed to counterattack the enemy. Truth affirmations are a *part* of the process of breaking strongholds, but they are not the whole of it.

No, not one of these three efforts—prayer, dependence on the Word, or speaking truth affirmations—is effective to combat the strongholds of Satan alone, but the *combination* of all three of them together will break the chains that have bound the most belligerent of strongholds in believers' lives. We have to learn to combine effective prayer; biblical memorization, meditation, and confession; and daily positive affirmations to destroy permanently any stronghold the enemy has created in our hearts.

Effort #1: prayer

The devil has a few weaknesses, and the first one is that he must submit to the name of Jesus. When we pray in the name of Jesus, we exercise our heavenly rights to converse with the God of the universe. When we petition the throne room of God in prayer, we seat ourselves where the Word of God tells us we belong: next to Jesus (safe and sound). Ephesians 2:4–7 reads, "But God, who is rich in mercy, because of His great love with which He loved us, even when we were dead in trespasses, made us alive together with Christ (by grace you have been saved), and raised us up together, and made us sit together in the heavenly places in Christ Jesus" (NKJV). We are given authority to speak with God about anything as His very own child. He hears us and doesn't turn a deaf ear to us, just as He wouldn't do that to Jesus. Jesus says as He is praying to the Father in John 11:42: "I know that You always hear Me" (NKJV).

Jesus's prayers are always heard by the Father, and because we are seated with Him in heavenly realms, we are also joint heirs with Christ. The Word says: "Now if we are children, then we are heirs—heirs of God and co-heirs with Christ, if indeed we share in his sufferings in order that we may also share in his glory" (Rom. 8:17). Because of our seat and because of our new birthright as a child of the Most High, when we pray, He always hears us. Our prayer rights are what we exercise first in our fight to break satanic strongholds.

There is power in the name of Jesus. Philippians 2:9 says: "Therefore God exalted him to the highest place and gave him the name that is above every name." In John 14:13 Jesus says, "I will do whatever you ask for in my name." That is powerful. The word *whatever* includes satanic strongholds being broken. Prayer in the name of Jesus Christ is powerful and effective in beginning the demolition of satanic strongholds in your life. It brings Jesus into the picture, and when Jesus shows up, the devil's going down!

Effort #2: Scripture

Second, the devil has no comeback for a soldier armed with the Word. Demons have to flee when we fight with real weapons of warfare: the sword of the Spirit, the helmet of salvation, the breastplate of righteousness, and feet fitted with the readiness that comes from the gospel of peace (Eph. 6:10–18). My fellow warrior, it is called the gospel of *peace* for a reason. We are supposed to rest in that peace, and our confidence comes from none other than Jesus Christ and the power of His Word!

Psalm 119:45 reads, "I will walk about in freedom, for I have sought out your precepts." Living in the truth of God's Word brings freedom. The kind of freedom I am talking about is worth the work needed to obtain it. You will have to submit control. You will have to figure out in your heart of hearts that it is better to live one moment the way God ordained you to live than a lifetime of demanding your own way.

Freedom begins when we take the Word of God and we begin to fight the enemy with truth. Jesus calls Himself the Way, the Truth, and the Life. We begin to figure out what is true in our lives by getting to know Truth Himself: Jesus. And we get to know what is true by studying the Word. They will be one and the same, because Jesus is the Word made flesh. Getting to know God's Word helps you get to know Jesus better. But, even better, speaking the Word of God out loud helps you to stay in truth.

In 2 Corinthians 10:3–5 we learn:

> For though we live in the world, we do not wage war as the world does. The weapons we fight with are not the weapons of the world. On the contrary, they have divine power to demolish strongholds. We demolish arguments and every pretension that sets itself up against the knowledge of God, and we take captive every thought to make it obedient to Christ.

We demolish any arguments and pretensions that set themselves up against the Word of God. When we begin to take our Bible study seriously and realize what God's Word says about different situations, we know that if there is something we are thinking that we can't find in God's Word about life or about people or about us, it's most likely something we're not to be thinking about. It's a lie! It's a trap, and we need to take it captive before it traps us.

Effort #3: truth affirmations

So how do we take a thought captive? That's where the third effort comes in. We start with a quick affirmation. When we catch ourselves thinking something we shouldn't be, we need to say our stance on the thought out loud to ourselves, to the enemy, and to the principalities of darkness. Sometimes it's a simple no. I like to say, "No, devil! I will not be offended, and I will not offend anyone! Help me, Jesus."

After we have affirmed our stance, our next step is to replace that lie with a truth. Now it really depends on what the ugly offense is that the enemy is trying to put on you. Maybe you've already asked forgiveness for something but can't shake the guilt and condemnation you are feeling. After saying, "No, devil. I will not be offended, and I will not offend anyone! Help me, Jesus," tell yourself, "I am the righteousness of God in Christ Jesus. I will be victorious where my thinking is concerned. I can do all things through Christ! I have the Holy Spirit. I have self-control. I have a sound mind." Tell yourself these truths each day, first thing out of bed if you have to. Beat that enemy to your thinking and to your feelings with affirmations of truths from God's Word.

This is where our dependence on Scripture comes into play again. I pull up Scripture and put it out there for the real healing to happen. I say, "Therefore, there is now no condemnation for those who are in Christ Jesus" (Rom. 8:1). Or I say, "Not that I have already obtained all this, or have already arrived at my goal, but I press on to take hold of that for which Christ Jesus took hold of me. Brothers and sisters, I do not consider myself yet to have taken hold of it. But one thing I do: Forgetting what is behind and straining toward what is ahead, I press on toward the goal to win the prize for which God has called me heavenward in Christ Jesus" (Phil. 3:12–14).

Sometimes one scripture will be enough, but if you are like me, I usually need two or three power-packed scriptures to get me through a little attack of the enemy on my mind. I then begin to pray and thank God that, by the power of His Word, I am more than a conqueror, and I praise Him and thank Him and present my heart to Him. Sometimes I am alone, and I can speak out loud to Him, but a lot of the time I'm out in public and have to silently or quietly pray to myself.

Again, as I've said every step of the way, you have to be committed to working these strongholds out. You have to be willing to do some work. We can't just sit back and allow the enemy to take our thoughts captive. We are in control of our thoughts, and we need to make them obedient to Christ.

Our brains are such complex organs. If we allow the enemy to rule us in our thinking, he has entrance to do what he wants. Shut the door on him, though, and watch those strongholds begin to tear down. I dare you to start feeling peaceful! I dare you to go a whole day without fear, or anxiety, or guilt. I dare you to experience joy like you have never felt before. You can and you will, but you have to start by filling your heart with the Word.

Here is what the Word says: "Be on your guard; stand firm in the faith; be courageous; be strong" (1 Cor. 16:13). First Corinthians 15:58 says, "Therefore, my dear brothers and sisters, stand firm. Let nothing move you." In Ephesians 6 when we learn how to put on the full armor of God, it says to do this "so that you can take your stand against the devil's schemes" (v. 11) and so that "after you have done everything, to stand" (v. 13). Have you done all that you can do? Have you made a decision to be dedicated to your healing and deliverance?

Let's Get Disciplined

My niece loves competitive dance. Sometimes I watch her dance and am in awe of her skills. She practices daily and attends a class six days out of seven. She is dedicated to dance, and her dedication shows on stage. There are also girls at the recitals who attend only a weekly class. Their routines are obviously more elementary than hers, and this is not to say one level of dance choice is superior to the other. I am simply pointing out that your mastery of anything will not come unless you are fully dedicated to it. This goes for everything—from dance to schoolwork to freedom from the enemy. My niece also knows that she better not show up to dance class without her dance shoes, leotard, or other dance supplies. Her teacher will send her home. Friends, the enemy will send you packing too, if you show up to fight him without your armor on.

When we fight the way God calls us to fight in order to break satanic strongholds in our lives, we become stronger and more confident in the sureness of our deliverer. Every time we fight the good fight of faith and we can turn around and peace is flowing like a river, I believe angels are celebrating in the supernatural and a scoreboard in heaven shows us as more than conquerors.

Know this: you should never be waiting around for an attack to come. I promise you, it will come. You have to be praying God's Word over your life and your family and your situations and your jobs and your vehicles and your friends and your neighbors—over your everything.

You have to memorize Scripture. We cannot live outside the pits of our lives without knowing God's Word like we know the Pledge of Allegiance, like we know our Social Security Numbers, like we know our PIN numbers. Make God's Word important to you, my friend. As Proverbs 23:23 says, "Buy the truth and do not sell it."

And we have to pray. We can't just listen to workshops about prayer, find books on how to pray effectively, or buy prayer journals. Instead we need to make time every day to actually be in prayer and talk to God. Pray little prayers to Him all day long to keep yourself in peace. Pray over your kids. Pray over your spouse. Pray over your loved ones. Be a prayer warrior to become free. Talk to Him like your best friend.

Going back to that passage in 2 Corinthians 10:3–5, it says, "We do not wage war as the world does.... We demolish arguments and every pretension that sets itself up against the knowledge of God, and we take captive every thought to make it obedient to Christ." A word in there jumps out at me when I read it, and it's the word *we*. *We* wage war. *We* demolish arguments. *We* take captive thoughts. Here's your first lesson: if you want to break the enemy's strength in your life, you must take the first step. You have to fight your own fight. You have to wear your own armor. Pastors, Bible teachers, and ministry leaders can hand you the armor, but you have to put it on! You have to fight your own fight with your own gear.

You must confidently stand firm with your feet fitted with the readiness that comes from the gospel of peace. You have your armor on, my friend. You will be fine. Fight the enemy with truths. He has no ammunition; he only has lies. *You* have the truth.

Truth, affirmations, God's Word, and prayer are the ingredients needed to destroy strongholds in your life. You have to fight your own fight, but this is the truth: "No temptation has overtaken you except what is common to mankind" (1 Cor. 10:13). All around this world your brothers and sisters are fighting the same fight. You have the same weapons they have. But few will stand in the victory that God desires us to stand in because the enemy has tricked them into believing it's not going to end well. We know better. We know the enemy's time is numbered. We know our daddy rides in on a white horse in the end, and we will be riding beside Him in white robes of righteousness. And what a glorious day that will be!

I Feel, I Feel, I Feel

Have you ever realized how driven we are by our feelings? I am blown away sometimes at my own flesh and how one day I can be so gung-ho for something, then the next day, not so much. It is obvious how dangerous it can be to rely on our feelings. Our feelings change like the temperature in Florida in winter—flip-flop weather one day, winter boots and coats the next.

Today I had to literally push myself through

my morning chores, my exercise routine, and my designated research time that I have mapped each day. I really don't even know what my flesh felt like doing. It just didn't want to do anything it was supposed to. So, I pretty much crucified it and made it obey my Spirit.

Do you know that you will end up being a slave to sin or a slave to righteousness? It truly is your choice, but you are a slave to something. If we remember that our feelings don't get a vote, we will be more likely to live a life worthy of our righteousness. Otherwise we will bounce back and forth, tossed by waves of joy and guilt depending on our mood that day.

We have to remember that the only truth that we can rely on is God's Word. Everything else is fickle and unreliable. Everything else lands in gray areas. But God's Word is pretty black and white and easy to comprehend. Everything else says, "If I feel like it." God's Word says, "Let it be."

Today we can make a choice to set our minds and keep them set on things above and not on whatever we feel like. Because I am pretty sure—yes, positive—that Jesus didn't want to go to the cross for our sins. He even asked God if there was any other way. But He immediately caught Himself in His feelings and said, "Not My will, but Yours."

http://momydlo.wordpress.com
/2014/01/15/i-feel-i-feel-i-feel/

Homework

Spend time in prayer as you answer the following questions.

1. *What is a stronghold?*

2. *How does the devil create strongholds in our lives?*

3. *What is an offense? Are you easily offended? How can you protect yourself from being offended by the enemy of your soul, Satan?*

4. *What three spiritual ingredients, used together, can be effective in breaking down strongholds from the devil?*

5. *How can you protect yourself from the tactics of the devil?*

Read the following scriptures and rewrite them in your own words:

- Luke 10:17–20

- 1 Corinthians 16:13

- 2 Corinthians 10:3–5

- Ephesians 6:10–18

Memorize

We demolish arguments and every pretension that sets itself up against the knowledge of God, and we take captive every thought to make it obedient to Christ.

—2 Corinthians 10:5

Confession

Practice saying out loud over and over this week: "I have control over my thoughts. I am free, in Jesus's name!"

Application

Practice using the three components of prayer, Scripture memorization and meditation, and positive affirmations based on the Word of God to loose every chain that is binding you. Practice using these three tools all day long.

Journal Time

This week tell God how badly you desire to feel the freedom that He died for you to experience.

Chapter 7

STAY IN THE MOMENT

TOMMY AND I have been married since before I can remember. I literally have trouble thinking of my life before we became one in marriage. He's my best friend and partner in leading souls to the Savior.

Since Tommy is a salesman, his career requires that he travel sometimes. The truth is, I hate when he has to take a business trip. His travel and time away from home used to cause me to fear, dread, and have many sleepless nights. It used to bother me weeks out before a trip, and I wouldn't know how to control my dread. While Tommy was gone, the demands on me as a single parent added to my melting pot of negative emotions. I literally annoyed both of us with my fear, but I couldn't figure out how to stop my behavior. I was what I like to refer to as a "hot mess." By the time Tommy would return home, we both were more exhausted by my anxiety and fear than we were by the physical demands of travel.

Can you relate? Do you feel like an emotional burden on others sometimes? I can honestly say at one point or another I have seen how my fears and controlling behaviors have affected many of the people I love the most. Truly I say to you, that is the very reason I have worked so diligently to break free from anxiety. I am determined to draw a blood line in the sand and say, "Negative emotions will not control my children."

The "What If" Trap

As I look back now, I realize that the most tormenting thoughts I had did not take place while Tommy was gone. It was the *anticipating* dread that I struggled with before he would leave that stole my joy the most. I had a difficult time enjoying quality time with my husband during the week or weeks leading up to a trip because I was preoccupied with the dread of the trip that was coming.

Dread is an important topic for us to touch on here. It is a very similar emotion to fear. If we dread something, it's almost as if we have lived it out completely with the worst-case scenario coming to pass. I have heard it said that when you dread something, it's like doing it twice. We usually walk through an experience once with God, and He gives us the grace we need to deal with that experience as it happens. But with dread our minds believe God's grace won't be present to assist us in handling it, and we're playing out this idea even before we walk it out.

The truth is, God's grace is alive and active in the present moment, and His grace is sufficient for us to be able to handle whatever we must face. God is not going to pour out His grace on us in our poor thinking patterns, such as dread. He will not work against His Word, and His Word specifically says, "Do not worry about tomorrow. Tomorrow will have enough worries of its own." (See Matthew 6:34.)

Worrying about the tomorrows in life or focusing on the what-ifs in every situation will steal your joy quicker than you can say *ulcer*. But worrying about tomorrow is a huge problem for those of us with control issues. We try to avoid the pain of a situation by attempting to think out every possible negative thing that could happen so we can guard ourselves from that outcome. But the truth is, we are not even guaranteed tomorrow. We could never guess on our most observant of days what is actually in store for us then. Tomorrow belongs to God. He controls it. His grace is only poured out to help us with today.

So how do we train ourselves to not worry about tomorrow? Literally we have to practice the same technique we learned in taking captive the enemy's lies and immediately replacing them with truth. We must remember again that the Word says, "We demolish arguments and every pretension that sets itself up against the knowledge of God, and we take captive every thought to make it obedient to Christ" (2 Cor. 10:5).

Worrying about or dreading tomorrow is exactly opposite of what God's Word teaches. It actually sets itself up *against* God's Word. So when we catch ourselves focused on the what-ifs of tomorrow, we need to take those thoughts captive, tell ourselves no, and immediately replace those thoughts with truth—truths such as, "Cast your cares on the Lord, for He cares for you" or "Do not worry about tomorrow" or "This is the day that the Lord has made; I will rejoice and be glad in it." If your thoughts are not focused on your present-day circumstances, you are wasting your time focusing and dwelling on those thoughts, and you need to take them captive.

Of course, in the case of planning for the future or setting goals or organizing thoughts and events, we must focus our thinking on tomorrow and the future temporarily, but we cannot become preoccupied with these thoughts or they can make us anxious. I love what Proverbs 19:21 says: "Many are the plans in a person's heart, but it is the LORD's purpose that prevails." Being a planner is a good and godly thing, but we have to learn to be OK when God decides to change the road map. After all, He will have His way, whether we fight it or not.

The "If Only" Trap

So we know now that we have to stop fearing and dreading tomorrow, but what if our true struggles are hung up in our yesterdays? What if we cannot let go of the past, and it is stealing our joy daily? I want to introduce you to a beautiful little word called *forgiveness*.

Harboring unforgiveness in our hearts is like a hacking cough that never seems to subside. You may get short breaks from it in your thinking, but the tiniest tickle brings it right back in full force. If we cannot learn to move past the hurt that someone caused us or the hurt that we caused someone else, we will struggle to stay in the moment of today and never enjoy the precious gift of peace that God so desperately wants us to have. Guilt and condemnation—whether directed outwardly or inwardly—is like a "Do Not Enter" sign for peace.

Guilt is triggered by some sort of shameful experience or thought that has slowly dug a pit of condemnation in our hearts. The truth is, we could step out of this pit at any time if we truly practiced forgiveness and finally put the past in the past and moved on.

Does that mean we bury our hurts alive? Goodness, no! We cannot ignore the pain of the past. We have to address it head on with the Lord, and sometimes with a trained counselor, in order to move on. In order to heal from any kind of infection, even if it is a stronghold of the mind, we have to get to the root cause and take it straight to Jesus to heal, instead of putting a bandage over it and expecting it to disappear. Hurt buried alive resurrects every time.

Jesus must take part in every detail of our pain in order for true healing to take place. We must work through our unforgiveness with Jesus and with the help of the Holy Spirit and His Word. Then we can begin to let go of the past once and for all. Sometimes recovery programs in our communities can be an amazing way to break free from hurts in our pasts. However you choose to work through your unforgiveness with the Lord, do it now and you will break the enemy's chains that have been holding you. Then you can learn to move past the if-onlys and learn to stay in the moment with Christ. The past is literally in the past, and the only control we have over our pasts is not letting it control our today.

Let me give you an example of what it looks like to live out both parts of this—the regret over something that happened in the past and the forgiveness we need to bring to such an experience. I recently spoke at a women's Mother's Day brunch and enjoyed the breakfast and the games and giveaways, but the truth is, I didn't give one of my best messages. When I showed up and realized it was a comical, giddy theme, I realized my message would be a little deep to take in while half of them were in costumes. Between the fact that I gave the message right after give-aways and games happened and the fact that I hadn't wor-shipped before I spoke, it felt a lot like Mo was speaking and not the Holy Spirit inside of me.

The women were gracious. They applauded, compli-mented, hugged, and thanked me afterward. But the perfectionist demon inside me kept replaying the entire event and reminding myself how awkward I felt most of the time.

You see, when I am giving a message in the Spirit, I could preach all day and never feel tired. But when I feel myself performing and teaching out of my own efforts, I feel exhausted and can't get off the stage quick enough.

I went home and I could barely talk. I was disappointed. I wanted to turn back time and present a better message. I was mad at myself—and a little at the coordinator for not checking my message against the theme. I fretted about the event for a couple hours. Then all of a sudden it hit me. The past is in the past. I had to go and get quiet before the Lord and repent!

You see, when I am talking about forgiving others and yourself so that you can truly live in the present and experience the grace and peace of today, I am not only speaking of life-changing hurts. It may just be literally letting go of yesterday's mess up so you can start fresh today. If we truly believe that God's grace and mercy rests in the present situation for every Christian because of the indwelling of the Holy Spirit, then that trust should help us to pursue a life focused on today.

All That's Real Is Today

A phrase God once supernaturally gave me is "Trust and obey; all that's real is today." You see, the if-onlys of the past and the what-ifs of the future have a way of robbing us of our today. We can become so preoccupied with the guilt of our yesterday and the mystery of tomorrow that we miss the present-tense joy God is trying to shower us with today. We have no power over the past but to forgive others or ourselves and we have no power over the future but to trust God and obey Him. Then we can actually begin to recognize that "if God is for us, who can be against us?" (Rom. 8:31). We can actually be free to abide in the present, knowing God's grace is sufficient to get us through anything we may face. We can begin to live peacefully, with a spirit of confidence, knowing that no matter what has happened or may happen, God will never take His love from us. Never—not ever!

Do you struggle with a fear of your past mistakes catching up with you and ruining your life? If so, you are in good company. Many of us are tormented by imagining worst-case scenarios happening because of something we did or maybe even imagined we did. Ephesians 5:8–9 says, "For you were once darkness, but now you are light in the Lord. Live as children of light (for the fruit of the light consists in all goodness, righteousness and truth)."

We will continue to perpetuate our poor decisions of the past or even our poor interpretations of what happened in the past if we continue to focus our thoughts on anything but living righteously today. The Word says that we are light, and when the light shines the truth of God's Word on situations, darkness and lies disappear. In order to step out of a twister of fear emotions that are swirling and attempting to drag us down, we must begin to saturate ourselves in the light of God's Word and focus on staying in the immediate moment. His Word allows us to see what is real.

Be Still, Be Here

Now let's get real. Many of our problems with anxiety stem from impatience. We are impatient creatures. We want our food now. We want our money quickly. We want our computers and phones to respond immediately. We want our cars to go faster. We surely do not want to wait on the Lord for our healing, deliverance, and marching orders. I mean, sometimes God makes us wait too long. Amen? And the worst is when God's answer to our prayers is "Not yet."

Why is God so dead set on teaching us patience? Why must we be still and wait patiently, as the psalmist explains? He says, "Be still before the LORD and wait patiently for him" (Ps. 37:7). I can answer this question with another scripture. Psalm 46:10 says, "Be still, and know that I am God." Patience teaches us that God is God, and we are not.

I know plenty of anxiety-ridden people, including myself, who have had to learn the hard way that our ways are not always the "perfect" way to do things. Quite honestly I usually have a three-part plan on how to fix everyone's lives. Can I get a witness? My friend, the truth is that my control issues are exactly what are keeping me from experiencing God's perfect peace. My control issues put themselves on the throne of my heart, when the only One who belongs on that throne is Jesus. Patience in its most beautiful form puts God back on His throne, puts to death our imaginary agenda, and allows peace to flow in our hearts where once only worry and fretting resided. God teaches us to be still and wait for our own good:

> Now listen, you who say, "Today or tomorrow we will go to this or that city, spend a year there, carry on business and make money." Why, you do not even know what will happen tomorrow. What is your life? You are a mist that appears for a little

> while and then vanishes. Instead, you ought to say, "If it is the Lord's will, we will live and do this or that." As it is, you boast in your arrogant schemes. All such boasting is evil."
>
> —JAMES 4:13–16

Oh my goodness! Is God saying here that my to-do lists are evil? If yes, I'm in a lot of trouble. Of course He's not. God is a god of organization and order. He desires that we make plans and set goals and work diligently toward those goals. But if those goals and plans become stumbling blocks to God's plans, we'd better be prepared to let them go. Let them go! Let go of whatever your controlling spirit wants to hang on to with a vice grip and handcuffs. Let it go so God can teach you the patience you need to obtain in order to remember that God is God, and we are not.

Trust and obey; all that's real is today.

Preach Yourself Happy

It was a normal Thursday morning at the Mydlo house. My high schoolers were already out the door. Tommy was showering in one bathroom to get out the door to work. Jake was stirring in his room, preparing for his morning college classes, and Eli was in the shower, preaching himself happy.

I was rounding up socks and shoes for Eli, and I couldn't help but overhear him through the bathroom door. So I stopped what I was doing and listened. I could hear him saying this: "No, devil, you are trying to ruin my joy today. I am excited to go to school. I like school. It's my day to go see Mrs. Stewart [his reading tutor]. I love going to Mrs. Stewart's class. Who would have thought learning could be fun too?"

Then quiet came. Then he started again. "I love lunch and PE!" Before I knew it, he was in there singing in the shower.

I have to tell you, I was tearing up. I thought to myself, "You got it, baby. Put that devil back in his place, and live free and joyfully."

It made me realize something all over again, even though I have seen it a million times. The Holy Spirit showed me again that the best sermons are those lived out right in front of people. Eli learned how to take hold of the peace that Jesus wants him to have by watching me do it daily. Thank You, Lord, for every time I have struggled in front of my kids. Now they don't have to.

http://momydlo.wordpress.com
/2013/11/14/preach-yourself-happy/

Homework

Spend time in prayer as you answer the following questions.

1. How often does a spirit of dread attack your thought life?

2. How can you work to stop dreading situations or events?

3. What steps can you take to plan for the future but not become fearful or obsessed about those plans?

4. Take an emotional inventory. Are you harboring unforgiveness for anyone, including yourself? If so, take time right now to get into prayer with God and begin the process of forgiveness once and for all. If you need help with this process, perhaps pray about searching out a counselor at your church or joining a support or recovery group in your town.

5. What is going on in your life right now that is joyful and beautiful? Take some time to thank God specifically for those things. Meditate on them for a few minutes.

Read the following scriptures and rewrite them in your own words:

- Isaiah 43:18
- Matthew 18:12–14
- Philippians 3:12–14
- Colossians 3:13
- Matthew 6:34

Memorize

Give us today our daily bread.

—Matthew 6:11

Confession

Practice saying out loud over and over this week: "Trust and obey; all that's real is today."

Application

Make an effort to recognize every time you are dreading anything, whether big or small, and say out loud, "I will not dread."

Journal Time

This week continue to write in your thankfulness journal. Record your anxious thoughts so that you can test whether they are hang-ups from the past or fears of the future. Then ask God to cover you in His grace during your present situation. His peace comes when we can stay in the moment.

Chapter 8

SERVING HELPS

IN THIS CHAPTER we are going to talk about getting your mind off yourself and onto others. God calls us to take care of the needy, feed the poor, clothe the naked, and lead the captives to freedom. Why do you think God has chosen to use us? God, in all of His infinite power, could in one second snap His fingers and change everything—literally all the hunger could be wiped away, orphans could be housed, widows could have new husbands, and pain could disappear. The God we know and trust could do that. I believe that. But why doesn't He? Why does He allow the suffering in this world to happen? Why does He allow children to die of sickness and disease, child abuse to take place, and people to die of hunger? Why does He allow it, my friend?

I am going to tell you what I know of an answer to this from what I know about our God through studying His Word and watching Him move in my life, and it's this: He uses pain and struggle to draw all men unto Him. He uses our hurts, habits, hang-ups, sadness, sickness, tears, trials, loneliness, grief, and, yes, even anxiety to pull us near to Him.

God cares so much more about our eternal salvation than our day-to-day comforts that He will allow bad things to happen to good people and strongholds to be developed so that His glory can be revealed when we finally break free. Jesus even tells His apostles, "In this world you will have trouble. But take heart! I have overcome the world" (John 16:33). He pretty much promises us problems. Have you ever heard people say, "Where there are people, there are problems"? Well, I am going to take that one step further and tell you that where there are God's people, there are answers to problems.

That is why churches are one of the only businesses you'll find that go against everything you have ever learned in economics class. When the economy is bad, fewer people go on vacations, fewer people go to theme parks or out to eat, fewer people buy stuff and build houses. But for some reason, when the economy is struggling, church numbers go up. More people fill the seats looking for answers to their questions. More people attend Bible studies to dig in and get some healing for their hurts. More people serve the needs of others because they know what it feels like to hurt.

God's economy is the opposite of the world's. The world says to hold on to it, because you might need it for a rainy day. God says to let some of it go so He can fill your cup until it overflows. Churches thrive, and God adds to His numbers of saints when times are tough. It's a simple kingdom fact. He allows us to hurt so we can eventually use that hurt to help others. He wants you to make your test your testimony. He wants to make beauty out of ashes.

Beauty From Ashes

There is nothing more beautiful than watching what happens in recovery and counseling ministries when people walk in with addictions, hurts, and pain, then meet Jesus, work through some biblical truths, and get set free—then end up leading small groups, ministering to others, and lifting others up. That is full-circle ministry.

There is nothing more beautiful than watching people come into a food pantry for groceries, work hard to get back to work, and get their finances straightened out—then turn around and donate food to the pantry for others who will need it. That is full-circle ministry.

There is nothing more beautiful than watching a good friend whose husband left her for another woman years ago allow God to be her husband, provide for her needs, and help her raise her children—then turn around to encourage other women who are facing divorce. I have a friend who went through this. She allowed God to give her strength to totally forgive her ex-husband and tell him she forgave him. Today they are talking almost every day, co-parenting beautifully, and working together instead of separately to make ends meet in a tough economy. Her ex-husband even spoke to her about feeling God take care of his needs and open doors. That is full-circle ministry.

There is nothing more beautiful than watching delivered addicts minister to youth before they ever pick up a drug, watching older mothers teach younger mothers how to raise their children in godly homes, and watching people who have spent time in prison turn around to minister in the prisons to the lonely and forgotten. These are full-circle ministries.

Max Lucado describes this beautiful exchange in his book *It's Not About Me.* He writes, "We'd see our suffering differently. 'My pain proves God's absence' would be replaced with 'My pain expands God's purpose.'"[1]

But how do we get there? How can we get strong enough in our hurt and pain to forgive people who have hurt us, love people who are unlovely, and make good out of so much bad? We get there only one way. We get there by pouring ourselves out and allowing God to fill us.

Poured Out in Freedom

It isn't enough to study the Word, pray on all occasions, and attend services regularly. Those things are all necessary to grow in Christ, but in order to get free of the bondage of anxiety, you have to get your mind off yourself. You've got to break the chains of selfishness and narcissism, and you have to become others-focused.

Personally I have been fellowshipping with other believers since I was a new Christian eighteen years ago. I have studied the Word and been a part of life groups and Bible studies. I have always been a worshipper. I've attended services regularly and tithed for the last fifteen years and have been extremely faithful in these things. I have seen the Lord bless us through it all.

But honestly nothing has helped me die to selfishness and pursue holiness like service work. Nothing has healed my heart of bitterness like remembering how the same people who hurt me most often served with me in the trenches of ministry, sweating together, working together, building together, crying together. Nothing has given me the power to forgive and move on from hurts and disappointment like serving the Lord with others and remembering those times that our service to the Lord was not in vain. God allows me to remember those times when my heart wants to be angry or bitter.

And God has shown me so many times that no matter how many scriptures we meditate on, songs we sing, or prayers we pray, sometimes the only way to get our mental and physical healing is by getting our minds off ourselves and getting our hands a little dirty.

This is not some self-help guru idea. It is biblical truth. Isaiah 58:6–12 says:

> Is not this the kind of fasting I have chosen:
> to loose the chains of injustice
> and untie the cords of the yoke,
> to set the oppressed free
> and break every yoke?
> Is it not to share your food with the hungry
> and to provide the poor wanderer with shelter—
> when you see the naked, to clothe them,
> and not to turn away from your own flesh and blood?
> Then your light will break forth like the dawn,
> and your healing will quickly appear;
> then your righteousness will go before you,
> and the glory of the LORD will be your rear guard.
> Then you will call, and the LORD will answer;
> you will cry for help, and he will say: Here am I.
>
> If you do away with the yoke of oppression,
> with the pointing finger and malicious talk,
> and if you spend yourselves in behalf of the hungry
> and satisfy the needs of the oppressed,
> then your light will rise in the darkness,
> and your night will become like the noonday.
> The LORD will guide you always;
> he will satisfy your needs in a sun-scorched land

> and will strengthen your frame.
> You will be like a well-watered garden,
> like a spring whose waters never fail.
> Your people will rebuild the ancient ruins
> and will rise up the age-old foundations;
> you will be called Repairer of Broken Walls,
> Restorer of Streets with Dwellings.

I get choked up reading this scripture because when I see, "You will be called Repairer of Broken Walls, Restorer of Streets with Dwellings," it makes me think of a repair and renovation ministry I led for six years. It was the local church's outreach to the community in which we provided safe shelter for those in need, food to those who were hungry, and clothes for the needy. "Repairer of Broken Walls, Restorer of Streets with Dwellings"—how I want God to look at me and smile and give me that name! How I desire for Him to call me helpful.

Don't we want to please God? Don't we want Him to look down and say, "That's My girl! She cares about what I care about. She hurts for what hurts Me and doesn't just talk about it. She does something about it." Of course we desire that. He's our dad. Every child is built with that desire to please their dad.

Our heavenly Father is pleased with us when we loose the chains of injustice, untie the cords of the yoke, and help set the captives free. But that is just the awesome recognition we will get when we are in heaven. What about right now? He blesses us now as well when we reach out to others. Verse 8 of the passage above reads, "Then your light will break forth like the dawn, and your healing will quickly appear." I believe you are going to get healed when you get outside your own misery and get focused on other people.

Verses 10–11 read, "And if you spend yourselves in behalf of the hungry and satisfy the needs of the oppressed, then your light will rise in the darkness, and your night will be like noonday. The LORD will guide you always; he will satisfy your needs in a sun-scorched land and will strengthen your frame." My friend, if we will get rid of our selfishness, this verse promises us joy when we feel depressed, satisfaction for our needs, and strong bodies. You can see from just this passage of scripture that God cares for those who care for others. He's got your back! But my favorite part is in verse 10, where it says, "Your night will be like noonday." Do you prefer noon to night? I know I do. He will make your nighttime as peaceful as noontime. That's good stuff.

Ephesians 5:1–2 says, "Follow God's example, therefore, as dearly loved children and walk in the way of love, just as Christ loved us and gave himself up for us as a fragrant offering and sacrifice to God."

Try the Opposite Action

How do we give ourselves to others? By getting our minds off ourselves and on others. We as Christians should understand this, but sometimes, unfortunately, our selfish nature keeps us bound in our own misery when we could be helping others and leading them to the one true Savior.

To help us out with this, let's consider an actual therapy approach called *opposite action therapy*. What this entails is when you recognize that your thinking is not quite in line with God's Word or that there is a pattern of thinking that is unhealthy, you are to do the opposite of what that feeling leads you to do.

Let me explain a little. Below are a few feelings and what our natural inclination would be to do when we feel them:

- Anger: lash out
- Sadness: isolate
- Fear: run away

Opposite-action therapy works when you've identified the emotions and you work on doing what's opposite. For example:

- Anger: gently avoid or be kind
- Sadness: be active and engaged
- Fear or anxiety: approach what makes you scared

Service work can help so much in this response of doing the opposite of what we feel. We will not feel like running out and feeding the homeless when we feel depressed. We will not feel like being a greeter at our home church when we feel anxious. We will not feel like volunteering in the nursery when we feel sad. After all, when we feel depressed, that selfish and self-centered voice keeps playing in our heads. Sometimes the only way to get that skipping record to turn off is to get your mind onto someone or something else. You do the opposite, and peace comes!

The truth is, we are not called to sit on our behinds in the pews, eat up good teaching, and become fat Christians on the Word. Amos 6:4–7 reads:

You lie on beds inlaid with ivory
and lounge on your couches.
You dine on choice lambs
and fattened calves.
You strum away on your harps like David
and improvise on musical instruments.
You drink wine by the bowlful
and use the finest lotions,
but you do not grieve over the ruin of Joseph.
Therefore you will be among the first to go into
exile;
your feasting and lounging will end.

I don't think I need to say in a stronger way that God doesn't want to hear you whining when you could be feeding, complaining when you could be encouraging, and moaning when you could be ministering. Yes, we are called to cast our cares on Him, but there is still a call, my friend. You need to get your mind off yourself. Die to self and your anxiety will die along with it. Work on loving people everywhere you go. If you see someone in line fumbling for their last penny to pay their bill in the grocery store, cover them. If someone needs to pull out in traffic and you have the right of way, let them go. If you're wearing an outfit someone says is beautiful, I challenge you to give it to them. Become obsessed with giving. Give of yourself in ways that you never have before. Wake up in the morning and ask God, "Who needs me today, Lord?" I promise, He will reveal someone to you. Just work on thinking about others and being a blessing, and before you know it, you are going to feel some peace.

Learn From Jesus

Now don't live in extremes, my friend. I am not telling you not to practice healthy boundaries and self-care, but I am telling you to think more about others' needs than your own. When you do, your life will change for the better. I can guarantee it. You will give, and it will be given back to you. It is a biblical law in effect. You are not to make service your God. You are to make service your declaration to God that you love Him and you know He loves you.

Jesus completely understood this concept. Let's learn from Him:

> When Jesus heard what had happened, he withdrew by boat privately to a solitary place. [What happened was John the Baptist, his cousin, was beheaded.] Hearing of this, the crowds followed him on foot from the towns. When Jesus landed and saw a large crowd, he had compassion on them and healed their sick.
>
> As evening approached, the disciples came to him and said, "This is a remote place and it's already getting late. Send the crowds away, so they can go to the villages and buy themselves some food."
>
> Jesus replied, "They do not need to go away. You give them something to eat."
>
> "We have here only five loaves of bread and two fish," they answered.
>
> "Bring them here to me," he said. And he directed the people to sit down on the grass. Taking the five loaves and the two fish and looking up to heaven, he gave thanks and broke the loaves. Then he gave them to the disciples, and the disciples gave them to the people. They all ate and were satisfied, and the disciples picked up twelve basketfuls of broken

> pieces that were left over. The number of those who ate was about five thousand men, besides women and children.
>
> —MATTHEW 14:13–21

Dear friend, Jesus was grieving in this story. He had just lost his cousin, and He knew He needed to get alone with God and work through His emotions. But after He gave it to God, what did He do? He returned to shore and began serving. The disciples came to Him and said, "Send these crowds away, so they can go somewhere and get some food." But what did Jesus say? "No, you give them some food. Bring them to Me." He could have easily said, "I just found out My cousin is dead. I need some time. Someone else help them." But He didn't. He worked out His own healing by getting His mind off Himself and onto others.

Remember that motto "What would Jesus do?" We are called to try to act like Jesus. There is a reason Scripture talks about working out your salvation with fear and trembling (Phil. 2:12). We need to work a little, and we need to do it the way Jesus did. Romans 12:21 says, "Do not be overcome by evil, but overcome evil with good." We need to know that love covers a multitude of sins (1 Pet. 4:8). I trust that God's Word is getting so engraved into your being that you are beginning to look like Jesus, talk like Jesus, and even smell like Jesus. Do you know that the Word says we will have the aroma of Christ? (See 2 Corinthians 2:15.) Unsaved people literally should know in their senses that there is something different about you. I pray that they do.

When I recognize myself getting into anxiety, I know I have to get to helping or loving someone else because anxiety is such a self-centered emotion, and we have to fight it by getting outside of ourselves. First, I work through the lies I am believing, rebuke the enemy, call on the Word, and stand firm. Then I get to serving. If I am home, I will go get one of my kids and say, "Want to play a game?" I will take my youngest son, Eli, outside and have a book picnic, or I will ask my daughter if she wants to go for a walk.

I have decided that Satan is not stealing any more of my life and time with my family, monopolizing my mind, or stealing my peace. So I heap burning coals on him when I turn around and make memories with my kids, spending extra time with them when he wants to torment me and steal my peace.

Before you know it, dear friend, when you do this, your heart is full of joy and your loved ones feel loved as well. If you don't have kids, bless your husband or bless your parents. If you are getting anxious and have to fight with some love, work through the lies, get in some truth, then go visit a lonely neighbor, take them some cookies, and have a cup of coffee with them. Call a friend you haven't seen in a while, or stop by a nursing home and love on some people who are so lonely they would be happy to just talk about the weather. You can be a blessing to anyone. Go to a store and help a stranger. The key is that you get outside yourself and love someone else.

Proverbs 14:31 says, "Whoever is kind to the needy honors God." Honor God with your life, and He will set you free, dear friend. It is a beautiful thing. Go practice opposite-action therapy. Do the opposite of what your feelings are telling you to do and specifically say to yourself, "I have the mind of Christ." Then go and act like Christ to a hurting world. Stomp on Satan by blessing others!

A Sacrifice of Praise

One morning Tommy and I woke up to a child standing over us who had experienced an obvious fever dream. Eli's words were coming out so quickly. He was not himself. I put my hand on him and realized, "Yep, he has a fever." I told him, "Baby, go lie on the couch. Let Mommy get you some Motrin. You can sit with me while I do my Bible study."

So Eli lay on the couch and eventually fell back asleep after the juice and Motrin kicked in—and then Sara's alarm and Tommy's alarm went off simultaneously. On to round two...

Tommy dragged himself to the couch after the double-shift he worked the previous day and just needed a half a cup of coffee before he could talk—but there was obviously no time for Dad's sipping. Sara needed a safety pin for her dress and help opening the vitamins. Then she dropped the milk, slurped the cereal she had made herself, and planted herself right in front of Tommy and Eli and me on the couch, all of whom were just trying to get two minutes to wake up.

On to round three. Here came Tyco. *Scratch, scratch, scratch.* She worked through her fight against her flea bath and medicine yesterday, then howled to go outside because with the windows open, she could hear every dog within twenty miles of the house and feels it is her responsibility to start the "all-dog alert" in the neighborhood.

Tommy looked at me over his just-barely-cracked devotional. We looked at Sara, Tyco, and Eli and just smiled a little.

I thought to myself, "OK, Lord, this isn't going to be the morning I receive any fresh revelation for ministry. Guess I'd better start getting ready for round four, because Travis and Jake have to get off to school and work too."

Then it happened: revelation!

I realized I'm blessed! I'm blessed to have a houseful of distractions from my Bible reading. I'm blessed to work at home so Eli doesn't have to go to school sick because I have no other option. I'm blessed to have a husband who works so hard at two jobs that he is a little overtired this morning. I'm blessed to have a home filled with noise sometimes, because I think in God's eyes, this noise sounds like a symphony of sounds that He created with His own hands. These sounds are the sounds of His masterpieces: my loved ones.

I began to worship Him with thankfulness.

Hebrews 13:15 reads, "Through Jesus, therefore, let us continually offer to God a sacrifice of praise—the fruit of lips that openly profess his name." Thank You, Jesus. My lips will always confess Your name!

http://momydlo.wordpress.com
/2014/02/04/a-sacrifice-of-praise/

Homework

Spend time in prayer as you answer the following questions.

1. *How are you serving God on a regular basis?*

2. *What anxious thoughts, if any, crop up at the thought of serving in some capacity?*

3. *How can you practice opposite-action therapy this week?*

4. *How did Jesus deal with grief?*

5. *In what ways can you overcome evil with good?*

Read the following scriptures and rewrite them in your own words:

- Isaiah 58:6–12

- Ephesians 5:1

- Romans 12:21

- Proverbs 14:31

Memorize

Do not conform to the pattern of this world, but be transformed by the renewing of your mind.

—Romans 12:2

Confession

Practice saying out loud over and over this week: "I will turn from evil and do good. I will seek peace and pursue it!"

Application

Pray about where God may have you serve someone else or in organized ministry.

Journal Time

This week continue to write in your thankfulness journal. Then talk to God about how to become more focused on others than on yourself.

Chapter 9

NEVER QUIT

DO YOU KNOW what I believe is the greatest accomplishment you can experience as a Christian? I don't think it's to build a worldwide ministry, pastor a megachurch, be seen by millions on television, feed the poor, help widows, or set captives free. Our greatest accomplishment as Christians isn't fostering or adopting the most orphans any one person has ever taken in or witnessing the most decisions for Christ any evangelist has ever seen. These accomplishments and blessings are all amazing and supernatural and extraordinarily ordered by God. But I believe the greatest accomplishment we can obtain as Christ followers and true disciples of Jesus Christ is the power to persevere—the ability to never give up!

I didn't say never mess up. I didn't say never screw up. I didn't say never trip up. We are humans, and we will fail and mess up sometimes. I said the power to never give up.

AN UNEXPECTED TEACHER

If I were a gambling woman, I would bet you never would choose the following passage to represent perseverance. But God totally revealed it to me, and I absolutely love His creativity:

> After the time of Abimelek, a man of Issachar named Tola son of Puah, the son of Dodo, rose to save Israel. He lived in Shamir, in the hill country of Ephraim. He led Israel twenty-three years; then he died, and was buried in Shamir.
>
> He was followed by Jair of Gilead, who led Israel twenty-two years. He had thirty sons, who rode thirty donkeys. They controlled thirty towns in Gilead, which to this day are called Havvoth Jair. When Jair died, he was buried in Kamon.
>
> —Judges 10:1–5

Powerful, right? Oh my goodness, mind-blowing stuff, right? I know what you're thinking: "Really, Mo? This is your lesson on perseverance? No story of Joshua, no story of Paul, no story of Jesus?"

Nope! It's all about Tola, son of Puah and Dodo!

Bear with me while we dig into this for a second. I want us to read two verses here. First, verse 2, which refers to Tola. It says he led Israel twenty-three years. And now let's look at verse 3 about Jair. It says he led Israel twenty-two years.

When I read this, do you know what the Holy Spirit said to me? He said, "Mo, can you preach My word and write and speak and help single mothers for twenty-two or twenty-three years?"

Listen, sometimes in ministry and in directing two nonprofits, I have to down an extra cup of black coffee just to get through a midweek grant-writing seminar. When I try to wrap my head around leading in full-time ministry for twenty-two years, I get a little anxious. I work very compulsively, and I have taught myself to stay in the moment with the Lord. I can't get hung up on the past or worry about tomorrow. I've learned "Trust and obey; all that's real is today." Amen?

But here we see that these men led twenty-two and twenty-three years. What else do we know about them? We know Tola's dad and grandfather were Puah and Dodo and that he lived in the hills. We know Jair had thirty sons, and they had thirty donkeys. That's pretty much all we're told from the scriptures about them.

Now I want to share with you what the commentary in my Bible says about these two men: "In five verses we read about two men who judged Israel for a total of 45 years, yet all we know about their rule is that one had 30 sons who rode 30 donkeys. What are you doing for God that is worth noting? When your life is over will people remember more than just what was in your bank account or the number of years you lived?"[1]

At first when I read this, because I am such a results-oriented person and love to knock things off of my to-do list and get as much accomplished in a short amount of time as possible, I agreed with the commentary. Then after a little prayer I thought, "No, I feel differently." I thought about something. Have you ever raised thirty sons? Ever cared for thirty donkeys? I have one really smart dog and no plants. I can't grow a darn thing, and if someone told me I had to keep thirty donkeys alive, I would have a panic attack. Oh, and then there are the thirty sons. My friend, you know those sons had daughters-in-law, and I am sure that half of them were annoying. (Did I just write that out loud?)

Jair had grandchildren, surely. You don't have thirty sons without a huge amount of grandchildren to follow. And I'm sure their kids needed date nights. I'm sure Jair did some babysitting for his grandbabies. I'll tell you, sometimes a two-year-old going through a stage can be tougher than fighting armed men in battle. Am I right?

We can't forget that these were real people. We sometimes read our Bibles like a history book and fail to remember these people were just like us. They had families—children and grandchildren. They had land and homes to care for, food to put on the table, and, to top it all off, no help from being filled with the Holy Spirit. Jesus hadn't come to the earth yet and freed them from their sins. These people were relying on their own efforts to keep God's law.

I need the Holy Spirit every second, every minute, and every hour to do what God has called me to do. I'm a hot mess without Him. I would've stunk as an Old Testament believer! The Holy Spirit is my lifeline.

After twenty-two and twenty-three years leading Israel, Tola and Jair finished their work. All through the Book of Judges God's people struggled. They would follow a great leader, keep God on His throne, and then fall back into their sin of idolatry and do evil in God's eyes. Then war would come. They would fight and lose loved ones and land, and they would cry out to God. He would feel sorry for them and send them another great leader to rescue them. They would do good for a little while, then turn back to their idolatry and sin, and then there would be war. This happened over and over.

But get this: not under Tola and Jair's rule! You know what they did during these forty-five years? They raised sons and they rode donkeys.

When I was reading this passage to Tommy, he said, "Donkeys are work animals." I thought, "Yes, they are."

Donkeys aren't thoroughbred horses or Lipizzaner stallions. Donkeys carry stuff, and they work. Praise God, usually hard work brings peace, and God does not forget our work. The Book of Hebrews says, "God is not unjust; he will not forget your work and the love you have shown him as you have helped his people and continue to help them. We want each of you to show this same diligence to the very end, so that what you hope for may be fully realized" (Heb. 6:10–11). How long? To the very end!

Learn to Persevere

If you are struggling with perseverance, may I encourage you to read the Book of James? James is a perseverance preacher. You know how sometimes people label people prosperity preachers or charismatic preachers? I say James is a perseverance preacher. He is so helpful to me when I feel like giving up in any fight. James 1:12, for instance, says, "Blessed is the one who perseveres under trial because, having stood the test, that person will receive the crown of life that the Lord has promised to those who love Him." The crown of life comes by perseverance.

This life will have trials. And let's face it: anything good and great and amazing and worth pursuing will not be easy. A godly marriage isn't easy. It takes work and prayer and dedication to never give up. Raising godly kids in a very negative world does not come easy. Overcoming anxiety biblically with or without the use of medication or other temporary fixes is not easy. We have to persevere. We have to say no to many things the world says yes to. We have to stand on a wall and say, "No matter how hard this gets, I won't quit." Please note: I am not advocating that you stop taking medication if you have been prescribed something from your doctor for anxiety. There are sometimes chemical imbalances in which people can truly benefit from an antianxiety drug. It is of course my heart's desire that I see you completely dependent on God for your healing and not on medicine, but in any instance or situation everyone is different. If you have made a decision to stop taking any type of medication, do not do so without consulting a medical professional and following their advice throughout the weaning process.

In 2 Peter 1:5–8 we read, "For this very reason, make every effort to add to your faith goodness; and to goodness, knowledge; and to knowledge, self-control; and to self-control, perseverance; and to perseverance, godliness; and to godliness, mutual affection; and to mutual affection, love. For if you possess these qualities in increasing measure, they will keep you from being ineffective and unproductive in your knowledge of our Lord Jesus Christ." In this passage notice that perseverance is sandwiched between self-control and godliness. I believe that is no coincidence. In order to persevere in overcoming anxiety, it takes self-control. But after you have persevered, you begin to radiate godliness. What amazing dividends for not giving up!

It takes self-control not to complain when you're struggling. It takes self-control not to turn to old idols and defense mechanisms when you're struggling. It takes self-control not to attempt to drink or smoke away your troubles when you're struggling. It takes self-control not to run to the local grocery store to buy a carton of ice cream and down it completely when you're struggling. It takes self-control to persevere, but we are children of the Most High God. We have the power to never give up!

The definition of *perseverance* is "patient endurance of hardship; persisting in a state of enterprise in spite of difficulties and discouragement."[2] Did you catch that? Perseverance means persisting in spite of difficulties. It isn't persisting when all the bills are paid, the kids are healthy, and the sun is shining on us at our condo on the beach. Perseverance doesn't get tested when we're on the mountaintop. Perseverance is perfected in the valley and the deserts of our lives.

God is the essence of perseverance. He could have ended it all when Adam and Eve messed up, or when the chaos in Sodom and Gomorrah was in full swing, or when King David cheated on his wife with Bathsheba, or when Paul was Saul, out there murdering Christians. God could have walked away from us at any minute, but He didn't. He persevered in love, and that is exactly what He wants from us.

We persevere and make a decision to never give up fighting the good fight of faith by keeping Jesus right in front of our eyes. Hebrews 12:1–3 says, "Therefore, since we are surrounded by such a great cloud of witnesses, let us throw off everything that hinders and the sin that so easily entangles. And let us run with perseverance the race marked out for us, fixing our eyes on Jesus, the pioneer and perfecter of faith. For the joy set before him he endured the cross....Consider Him who endured such opposition from sinners, so that you will not grow weary and lose heart." Friend, we have not endured to the point of our blood shed on the cross. Our mental trials are hard. They are difficult, but we are still here. And with our eyes set on Jesus, we can persevere.

So yes, I think Tola and Jair did what was right in God's eyes. They worked hard, they raised their families, they led God's people, and they finished well. They aren't listed in the Hall of Faith in Hebrews, but God listed them in His book for us to read and learn from.

Keep on Keeping on

How about we just never quit? In this book I have given you some different tools and ideas of how to use the Word of God to rest in the peace of God, and I pray that resting doesn't mean being idle. You cannot be idle and be in peace if you are an anxious person. You will have to practice the techniques, work out your salvation with fear and trembling, study like you have never studied before, and trust that this next step will lead you into the peace that passes all understanding.

You can't quit. You are going to have days that you are going to feel like that old, ugly devil just won't get off your back, but it's OK because now you know what authority you have in the name of Jesus. You can call on that name and rest in the fact that demons have to flee at the name of Jesus. When you are walking with the Lord, you have a power on the inside of you that can literally move mountains. But if you give up while God is weeding the garden of your heart, you will never get to see the fruit of your increase.

Do you trust that you have this power? Because it truly is all about trust. You can call on the name when you are under the attack of anxiety, poor thinking, and fear. You can call on that name and be escorted into the peace of God. Don't underestimate the power of the name of Jesus! The blood of Jesus gives us access into the presence of God, but we have to be renewed in our minds daily. You don't just renew your mind once. You have to renew your mind daily in the Word.

I can't study for you. I can study for myself, and God can give me a word in due season to share with you. I can get some revelation that can help you, but you have to work out your own healing with Him. You have to get very real with God about your strongholds, poor thinking patterns, and lies you have believed for so long, and you have to let Him heal you personally. He wants that personal time with you. He is our great physician. You have waited long enough in the waiting room for your healing. Get in there and see the doctor and get well.

It sounds silly, right? To think of your quiet time with God like seeing the doctor? Truly, though, I think renewing your mind is sort of like chiropractic adjustments. I can go to my chiropractor, and my doctor can put my spine back where it needs to be to keep my immune system working right and keep my frame healthy and ready to work hard without pain, but it is not a one-time thing. I will lift something wrong, sleep wrong, or turn just a certain way and need to get adjusted again. It is only by consistency in visiting the chiropractor and following his requests for my health regimen that I stay well. And it is only by consistency in the Word of God and in prayer and communion with Jesus that you will feel consistently healed and restored. As Joyce Meyer points out in her book *Never Give Up*, "You know by now that doing something the right way one time does not necessarily bring great reward. It is doing something right over and over and over that will bring the good result you desire."[3]

You may feel free and peaceful one day reading the Word, then the next day life happens. Someone hurts your feelings. Satan sets you up to steal your joy. Your feelings lie to you. Life happens, and you have to get adjusted again. You have to renew your mind each day.

You will have to get up in the morning and know that before you set your feet on the ground, Satan is going to try to invade your thoughts. He will try to make you think of all the junk you didn't reconcile the day before. He will purposely try whatever he can to set you up to get you down. You have to make a conscious effort to stay ahead of him every day. You have to be the one to drag that tired body out of bed, grab that cup of coffee, and get in your favorite Bible study chair to arm yourself with the Word of God. You have to get to that dwelling place with Jesus immediately and call on Psalm 91:1: "Whoever dwells in the shelter of the Most High will rest in the shadow of the Almighty." You can have a day ahead of you that is so busy and crazy, filled with a to-do list that is a mile long, and you can stay in that rest because you will stay under His wing.

Become the Noble Woman You Can Be

Let's look at Proverbs 31:10–31:

> A wife of noble character, who can find?
> She is worth far more than rubies.
> Her husband has full confidence in her
> and lacks nothing of value.
> She brings him good not harm,
> all the days of her life.
> She selects wool and flax
> and works with eager hands.
> She is like the merchant ships,
> bringing her food from afar.

She gets up while it is still night;
she provides food for her family
and portions for her female servants.
She considers a field and buys it;
out of her earnings, she plants a vineyard.
She sets about her work vigorously;
her arms are strong for her tasks.
She sees that her trading is profitable,
and her lamp does not go out at night.
In her hand she holds the distaff
and grasps the spindle with her fingers.
She opens her arms to the poor
and extends her hands to the needy.
When it snows, she has no fear for her household,
for all of them are clothed in scarlet.
She makes coverings for her bed;
she is clothed in fine linen and purple.
Her husband is respected at the city gate,
where he takes his seat among the elders of the land.
She makes linen garments and sells them,
and supplies the merchants with sashes.
She is clothed with strength and dignity;
she can laugh at the days to come.
She speaks with wisdom,
and faithful instruction is on her tongue.
She watches over the affairs of her household
and does not eat the bread of idleness.
Her children arise and call her blessed;
her husband also, and he praises her:
"Many women do noble things,
but you surpass them all."
Charm is deceptive, and beauty is fleeting;

> but a woman who fears the Lord is to be
> praised.
> Honor her for all that her hands have done,
> and let her works bring her praise at the city
> gate.

We have believed the lie for too long that we cannot be this woman. The list is just too long; it's too much to ask of one woman. She is not real. But I am going to tell you, it should be all of our goals to become the wife of noble character. It is a pursuit of excellence. I believe God is overjoyed when His children pursue excellence. His Word says, "Be holy, because I am holy" (1 Pet. 1:16). We are never going to be holy, but we are to be pursuing it our entire lives.

The wife of noble character is a working mother who owns her own business and cares for the needs of her children. Her husband is an elder in the church, and her home is a safe, warm place to come home to. She takes care of the needy. She provides for her servant girls with love. She buys and sells land, and in doing all this, she keeps herself beautiful. She is the epitome of excellence.

How does she get that way? The Word says, "She gets up while it is still dark." My friend, she does not drag herself out of bed after the kids wake her up. She doesn't sleep just long enough to get up with everyone else. She beats the devil to her day! She gets up and spends time with God, finding out how to do all she needs to do that day.

I truly believe the morning is filled with such amazing revelation from God because in the quiet we can hear that still, small voice that God speaks with and that becomes drowned out so easily once the craziness of the day starts. If you are not a morning person, I know this may sound like drudgery, but I promise you that once you get some freedom in Christ, no soft feather pillow can give you that comfort and no down comforter can replace the peace that passes all understanding. Once you get a taste of that peace, you will never want those old cheap substitutes anymore!

Verse 27 says, "She watches over the affairs of her household and does not eat the bread of idleness." Why do you think she stays busy? Have you ever heard the phrase "An idle mind is the devil's workshop"? To pursue the goals and will God has for your life, you have to move. You have to do something. You cannot just stay in bed or sit on the couch and say to God, "Give me peace, God. Take away my fears. Take my burdens." God calls you to do something.

Furthermore, God wants to see us desiring the things of Him so much that we will die to our selfish nature daily to get a piece of what He has for us. He wants us to take hold of His Word, devour it, and use it throughout every second of our day to fill up this God-shaped hole in our hearts that only He can fill. He wants to help us carry out His plan for our lives. That is why we are here—to live out His plan for our lives. We are commissioned to lead others to Him and to bring as many people to heaven with us as we can. His plan is to give us life in abundance.

Satan hates all of this. Satan wants nothing less than to steal God's glory. But if you stay close to the Father, my friend, he can't touch you!

Stay Close to God

In all this I am reminded of a hero in the Bible named Nehemiah. God called Nehemiah to rebuild the wall of Jerusalem. This was not a small task, and Nehemiah came up against some crazy opposition. In the same way any time you are going to do something great with God (and notice I said "with God" and not "for God"), you will get opposition from Satan. But Nehemiah was able to do what he set out to do because he stayed close to God. He did not set out on his task without staying close to God in prayer.

The story reads:

> Meanwhile, the people in Judah said, "The strength of the laborers is giving out, and there is so much rubble that we cannot rebuild the wall."
>
> Also our enemies said, "Before they know it or see us, we will be right there among them and will kill them and put an end to the work."
>
> Then the Jews who lived near them came and told us ten times over, "Wherever you turn, they will attack us."
>
> Therefore I stationed some of the people behind the lowest points of the wall at the exposed places, posting them by families, with their swords, spears and bows. After I looked things over, I stood up and said to the nobles, the officials and the rest of the people, "Don't be afraid of them. Remember the Lord, who is great and awesome, and fight for your families, your sons and your daughters, your wives and your homes."
>
> —NEHEMIAH 4:10–14

Nehemiah reminded the people to remember the Lord and to get out there and fight for what was important to them. God blessed the rebuilding of the wall because they first prayed, remembered Him, then took up their swords and fought for their lives. That, my friend, is the key. Draw your strength from God, then fight. You need to get quiet, then get to work.

While I was on vacation this year, God led me to the Book of Isaiah, and a certain scripture rang in my mind the entire week that I believe is the key to walking out what God has for us in any of our struggles or challenges in life. Isaiah 30:15 reads, "This is what the Sovereign LORD, the Holy One of Israel, says: 'In repentance and rest is your salvation, in quietness and trust is your strength.'" This is the key to victory, my friend. We have to repent and stay close to God to be saved. The word *rest* refers to staying. Those are just the first two steps to be accepted into the family of God: repent and stay close to Him. Then we still have to walk out our lives on this earth, so you will need to be strong. The second half of the passage reads, "In quietness and trust is your strength." Our strength to fight the devil and his schemes and to walk through this life victoriously comes from quiet time spent with God and trusting in Him.

We are guaranteed to win when we allow Jesus to go before us, but we have to be armed and fight. Colossians 2:13–15 reads, "When you were dead in your sins and in the uncircumcision of your flesh, God made you alive with Christ. He forgave us all our sins, having canceled the charge of our legal indebtedness, which stood against us and condemned us; he has taken it away, nailing it to the cross. And having disarmed the powers and authorities, he made a public spectacle of them, triumphing over them by the cross." He disarmed them, my friend. His demons have no ammunition! You are fighting an adversary that has already been defeated. He has no reign over you. Jesus paid the price on the cross. Draw your strength from Jesus, and fight!

From what source are we drawing our strength right now? From other idols? From other "little gods" we have created? Are we drowning out those voices or racking up credit or expecting our husbands to fix our problems or talking on that cell phone or chatting online when we could be talking to our Savior? If you want to be victorious and change your stinkin' thinkin', it is imperative that you talk to God more than you talk on the phone; that you worship Him more than you worship a social media account; that you study more than stress; and that you pray more than panic. Remember, "In repentance and rest is your salvation, in quietness and trust is your strength." Let's get quiet and trust Him so that we can be strong.

Let me show you through the Word why those other things won't work. The fuller text of Isaiah 30:15–18 reads:

> This is what the Sovereign LORD, the Holy One of Israel, says:
>
> "In repentance and rest is your salvation,
> in quietness and trust is your strength,
> but you would have none of it.
> You said, 'No, we will flee on horses.'
> Therefore you will flee!
> You said, 'We will ride off on swift horses.'
> Therefore your pursuers will be swift!
> A thousand will flee
> at the threat of one;
> at the threat of five
> you will all flee away,
> till you are left
> like a flagstaff on a mountaintop,
> like a banner on a hill."

> Yet the LORD longs to be gracious to you;
> therefore he will rise up to show you
> compassion.
> For the LORD is a God of justice.
> Blessed are all who wait for him!

You can run to these other things, and your pursuers will keep chasing you. But God longs to be gracious to you. He rises to show you compassion. Why we flee to other things, I don't know, because it says, "Blessed are all who wait for him!"

I don't know about you, but I want all of His blessings in my life. I want that peace. I want that strength, and I want that anointing on my life. I want it to be so strong that I can be like Nehemiah and build walls for Jesus that the world says are too big to conquer. You too are called to build some walls. We all have a calling on our lives. You have to get quiet to find out what it is, and then start building.

Keep It Balanced

Your healing needs to be all about balance. Don't be so idle that Satan can rule your thinking, but be still enough so that God can talk to you. Don't start building until you talk to God to get the plans, and then don't stop when adversity comes. You need to press on and let God move you, even when you don't feel like you can move any more. There will be times to be quiet and still, to get those words of wisdom, and there will be times to run downhill with Jesus. You may think that you are going to trip and fall, but you won't if He is carrying you. Just keep on running.

Only by spending the time in the Word like you need to will you figure out how to avoid extremes in your walk with Christ. You must truly try to avoid all extremes to maintain the healthy balance you need in life. As Patsy Clairmont states in *Under His Wings and Other Places of Refuge*, "Those who have been or are being held hostage by panic are people given to extremes. Finding balance will not be easy for us, but it is possible."[4]

As an illustration, I'll tell you about the time I was talking to some friends about the water I drink. It is from the alfalfa plant. It is so good for your body in many ways, and it tastes really good. I mentioned trying to get one of my friends to get on a probiotic so she could get her colon healthy, and as we were talking, my friend said, "What are you eating?" I said, "Oh, these? Pop-Tarts. I drink green water and take probiotics so I can eat Pop-Tarts sometimes."

I don't live in extremes, my friend. I eat apples *and* cookies. Balance!

So be still to get some peace, and then get moving so you won't be idle and a target for attack. Get a healthy balance of study, work, and rest and you will begin to feel some peace. Work is a beautiful thing. I know we talked about service work and how it is healing. It is so true. Do not be afraid to work. Ecclesiastes tells us, "There is nothing better for people than to be happy and to do good while they live. That each of them may eat and drink, and find satisfaction in all their toil—this is the gift of God" (Eccles. 3:12–13).

Finally, Let's Get Practical

You may have anxiety for the simple fact that your house is a mess, your car has fast-food wrappers all over it, and your lawn needs a good mowing. You may be running to doctors for anxiety meds when you should just be cleaning out a closet. Your clutter can make you crazy. I know this may seem silly, but it might be true.

Dear friend, do you know what I do? Each day after I have my quiet time and get my kids off to school, I spend a little while running through my house making beds, throwing in a load of laundry, loading the dishwasher, and picking up from the night before. Before I begin writing, my house is clean. Not because anyone will be there and see it (because my Border collie could care less if the beds are made), but because I need to feel peace when I am working. I want to be mom when my kids get off the bus, and I don't want to be distracted with dishes, laundry, and vacuuming at that point. My house requires a little of my attention every day so that I don't have to spend hours catching up. Again, I try to avoid all extremes in every area of my life.

Maybe you need to laugh. When was the last time you rented a good comedy and sat down with your husband and just laughed? We have kids, so we laugh a lot. My nine-year-old is just plain funny. He was in a talent show at church and his bit was called "So My Parents Are in Ministry." The Bible says that laughter is good medicine. Get a good, clean joke book and laugh. There are clean comics out there that you can listen to. We can't take ourselves too seriously. Life is funny. We need to laugh at it.

Maybe you need to get outside more. Do you know that just by looking up, you release serotonin, a chemical in your brain that makes you feel good? You should find a quiet spot each day to just sit there, look up to heaven, and give thanks and talk to God.

Do you know that ten minutes of straight sunlight each day will give your body all your daily requirement of vitamin D? When we are deficient in vitamin D, we don't think well.

Maybe you need to get on an exercise routine. The natural endorphins that are released from exercise make you feel good. Even a brief walk with the dog each day can make a huge difference in your moods and emotions.

Or open your blinds! Natural light in your house can change your entire outlook on the day.

Dear friend, let's try some of these practical techniques, avoid all extremes, and never quit. No matter what Satan throws at us, if we will just stay the course for Jesus, we have a testimony. Second Peter 3:9 says, "The Lord is not slow in keeping his promise, as some understand slowness." His timing is perfect. Hang in there, because your deliverance may be just around the corner.

What else have we learned here? We need to renew our minds daily, cast down our other idols, and break satanic strongholds. We must recognize lies and replace them with truth, fast from wrong thinking, fall in love and dwell in the Word of God, and buy the truth and not sell it. We have to call on the name of Jesus and be saved. We have everything we need to be free. Let's step out of those imagined prisons the devil wants us to think we are in, and enjoy every day of our lives.

As we learned from the witness of Hebrews 12:1–3, we need to press on with heaven as our finish line. It doesn't matter how we started, dear friend. It just matters how we finish. Finish well, so that when you stand before God—like we all will someday—He will say to you, "Well done, good and faithful servant."

A Morning Jog

I just took my sweet dog, Tyco, for a jog. I love jogging her in the morning for many reasons. Not only is she much more behaved after I wear her out on foot, but she seems to eat better, sleep better, and greet people a little less crazy when they pop in for a visit.

But more than jogging to keep my dog healthy, my morning walk/jog this morning had me meditating on spiritual things left and right. I become so grateful when I walk out my front door and hit the pavement on foot. I look around and notice God's beauty in the clear blue skies and the hot sun on my body mixed with the warm breeze a slight jog creates. I notice how neighbors' lawns are growing green and plush because of our summer afternoon rains. I follow butterflies and dragonflies and lizards as they rush to enjoy the morning sun as well. I am in awe of God's beauty and it never gets old, no matter how long I live in the same neighborhood.

I am reminded of Psalm 19:1, which reads, "The heavens declare the glory of God; the skies proclaim the work of his hands." I love thanking God for nature, but it doesn't end there. I begin thanking Him that my legs do what legs were made to do. I thank Him for my eyes that can look where I am going and take in His beauty. I thank Him for ears to hear pool fountains, birds singing, and wind whistling through tree limbs. I thank Him for my heart that ticks the way it is supposed to and, quite honestly, might be in better shape than it was in my twenties because I am an overcomer of fear and anxiety.

I return home and my water in my water bottle tastes better than other times during the day because I am so thirsty. Then I thank God for my air-conditioned home and my laptop to write of His amazing love. Well, that brings me to right now and the sweet shower I look forward to as I start my day.

You might want to take a jog outside today too. It's pretty supernatural!

http://momydlo.wordpress.com
/2014/06/20/a-morning-jog/

Homework

Spend time in prayer as you answer the following questions.

1. *How can you avoid extremes in your healing?*

2. Do you have areas that you need to declutter so you can focus on your healing?

3. How are you taking care of yourself physically?

4. Where are you still allowing Satan to beat you, even though he is unarmed?

5. How will you work through the techniques you learned in this book to allow the Word of God to set you free?

Read the following scriptures and rewrite them in your own words:

- Psalm 91:1

- Proverbs 31

- Nehemiah 4:10–14

- Isaiah 30:15

- Colossians 2:13–15

- Hebrews 2:14–18

- Proverbs 17:22

- 2 Peter 3:9

Memorize

> Therefore, since we are surrounded by such a great cloud of witnesses, let us throw off everything that hinders and the sin that so easily entangles. And let us run with perseverance the race marked out for us, fixing our eyes on Jesus, the pioneer and perfecter of faith. For the joy set before him he endured the cross, scorning its shame, and sat down at the right hand of the throne of God. Consider him who endured such opposition from sinners, so that you will not grow weary and lose heart.
>
> —Hebrews 12:1–3

Confession

Practice saying out loud over and over this week: "I have a sound mind. I will never give up!"

Application

This application will combine all the techniques we have worked through together. Make a date with God each day and spend time in His Word, becoming closer to Him than anyone else. Enjoy growing closer to the Lord and experiencing His peace as you practice these methods:

1. Renew your mind daily in the Word of God.
2. Go on a fast from worrying. When you make it one day, make it two days, and keep up the good work.

3. Turn off some of the distractions that keep you from spending necessary time in the Word and in prayer.
4. Cast your cares on the Lord. Leave them at the cross and do not pick them back up.
5. Replace negative thinking with the Word of God.
6. Recognize when you are being lied to, and cast down the lies, replacing them with truth.
7. Practice opposite-action therapy.
8. Overcome evil with love and become others-focused.
9. Say your confessions out loud every day.
10. Continue to journal your prayers and thankfulness each day.
11. Make a decision to stay in the moment—trust and obey; all that's real is today—and never give up!

Journal Time

Share your plans with God about how you will renew your mind daily in the Word of God. Tell Him how much you love Him.

To close out our time together in this study, would you allow me to pray for you?

Dear Lord,

I come to You in Jesus's name on behalf of every one of my new friends who read and worked through this study. I pray for supernatural strength to endure. I pray for miracles to happen that each and every one of us could never come up with on our most creative of days. I pray that You become so real to my friend as she spends an enormous amount of time with You and in Your Word. I pray for healing, restoration, and peace for every hard-working woman who reads this. I pray for joy that is in abundance until it overflows. I thank You. I praise You. I love You. In Jesus's name, amen.

It has been a joy sharing the truths in this book with you. Fight the good fight, and never give up allowing God's Word to set you free! I love you.

I Am Not Afraid

I am not afraid to open the blinds,
to see what today's giant mystery finds.
I am not afraid to turn off my mind,
to think about relaxing, just to unwind.

I am not afraid to plan, just to play,
to not have to worry what people will say,
to enjoy my children as they are today,
because this little is not how they always will stay.

I am not afraid to admit when I am wrong,
to tell my children that I hurt for so long.
But now I will sing them such a sweet song,
and I think they consider me that much more
strong.

I am not afraid to say that I'm me—
a flawed and imperfect believer who can see
that I'm not where I am really wanting to be.
But I'm better than I was before Jesus saved me.

NOTES

Introduction

1. Merriam-Webster.com, s.v. "commit," http://www.merriam-webster.com/dictionary/commit (accessed July 4, 2015).

Chapter 1
First Steps in Overcoming

1. Stormie Omartian, *Finding Peace for Your Heart: A Woman's Guide to Emotional Health* (Nashville, TN: Thomas Nelson, 1991), 150.

2. Charles F. Stanley, *Confronting Casual Christianity* (Nashville, TN: Broadman & Holman, 1998), 41.

Chapter 2
Casting Down Idols

1. J. Keith Miller, *Hope in the Fast Lane: A New Look at Faith in a Compulsive World* (New York: Harper Collins, 1990), 74.

Chapter 5
The Devil Is a Liar

1. *Life Application Study Bible*, New International Version edition (Wheaton, IL: Tyndale House Publishers Inc./Grand Rapids, MI: Zondervan, 1991), 2239.

2. Billy Graham, *Peace With God: The Secret of Happiness* (Nashville, TN: Thomas Nelson, 1984), 63.

Chapter 8
Serving Helps

1. Max Lucado, *It's Not About Me: Rescue From the Life We Thought Would Make Us Happy* (Nashville, TN: Thomas Nelson, 2004), 8.

CHAPTER 9
NEVER QUIT

1. *Life Application Bible*, New International Version edition, 400.
2. Ibid., 2479.
3. Joyce Meyer, *Never Give Up! Relentless Determination to Overcome Life's Challenges* (New York: Hachette, 2008), 237.
4. Patsy Clairmont, *Under His Wings and Other Places of Refuge* (Nashville, TN: Thomas Nelson, 1994), 62.

ABOUT THE AUTHOR

Mo Mydlo has been happily married to Tommy Mydlo for twenty-one years. They reside in the Central Florida area with their four children and their dog, Tyco. Mo was ordained into ministry and served for six years as the local outreach director for one of the fastest-growing Christian churches in the nation. Her new calling is to teach women how to renew their minds in the Word of God. Mo is also very active in her community, helping single mothers and their children as the founder and executive director of The Vineyard: A Single Moms Community Corp.

Mo is available to speak at women's groups, events, and retreats. For more information about her schedule, please visit her website at unforsakenministries.com.

You can also follow Mo online:

Facebook: www.facebook.com/UnforsakenMo

Twitter: twitter.com/momydlo

Blog: momydlo.wordpress.com

OTHER BOOKS BY MO MYDLO

Notes From a Titus Woman: The A–Z of Caring for Your Home and Family

I Go Before You: A Companion for Your Journey Through Emotional Healing

Keepin' It Real

The Grace Race

Perfect Love

These books are available at Amazon.com.